CONSTRUCTION
MILLIONAIRE SECRETS

CONSTRUCTION MILLIONAIRE SECRETS

PROFIT TOOL BELT

DOMINIC RUBINO

ISBN: 978-1-7773729-0-3

Cover Art: Jaira Mandal
Editing: Conor McCarthy
Typesetting and layout: Karl Hunt

CONTENTS

CONTENTS

CONTENTS

DEDICATION

To my wife, Diedre, for being the solid rock that I can rely on and the most positive, beautiful woman in the world.

To my daughter, Valencia, for showing me the beauty of art and the importance of losing yourself inside your creative Passions. *I love you zero, Bella.*

To my son Joseph—for keeping me laughing and holding me accountable for details. For being my buddy and the best fishing partner I could ever have. *I get to be your Dad, and I love it.*

To my dad, Joe, who only lives to take care of his kids—for teaching me the most important thing. *A man stands by his word.*

To my mother, Lena, who is pure love, and completely dedicated to our family.

To my friends—and you know who you are—for talking smack, for joking around, for pushing me to think bigger, and reminding me of the importance of having a beer every once in a while.

DEDICATION

To Cody, my business coach, for pushing me to think bigger, holding me accountable, and having a zero-tolerance BS filter.

To my clients, who I hold as friends, for honestly sharing their deepest thoughts, their greatest goals, their heaviest concerns, and their biggest wins with me as their business coach.

And, finally I dedicate this book to the great life that I have. I am the most fortunate guy in the world because I'm surrounded by people who love me and people I can trust.

FOREWORD

By Martin Hunter

Attitude beats everything else.

My name is Martin and that's how I see the world. And I've seen a lot of the world. I spent some time in the military going places and doing things that you might watch in movies. It's on those missions that I learned about the importance of attitude.

My military experience in leadership and organization has taken me to some pretty exotic places. I've lived in countries and on islands most people have never heard of, where heavy mining and resource extraction go on at a frantic pace.

Mining was my first chance outside of the military to see that attitude was still one of the most important factors for success outside of the service.

I was brought in to lead and optimize field operations in a dangerous, high risk, environment with lots of heavy equipment and far too many humans moving around.

As with most construction sites, there were a lot of different cultures on my team's roster.

Being a remote location on a remote island, things could get pretty rowdy—especially when the different groups got into disagreements.

"Attitude . . .", I thought to myself. *"How can I get this unruly group, who don't even speak the same language to get the right attitude? An attitude where they could work together safely to complete the task at hand?"*

So I started watching the leaders of these two groups. I watched the guys who said they were in charge—and I watched and saw the guys who were really in charge.

I paid attention and I put together a plan. Because this plan had to work for these two groups—or they might end up actually killing each other.

By watching their attitudes I found their motivations. It was in their motivations that I was able to bring them together in a way that everybody worked safely and we still pulled heavy stuff out of the ground with heavy dangerous equipment like we were supposed to.

A decade later I landed back in North America. On a dark, cold morning I walked into a new gym, looking for a new routine. That's when I met Dom. Actually that's when Dom met me.

You have to understand this class starts at 6 a.m. Bleary-eyed, people are standing there waiting for the drill sergeant-like instructor to get things started. But Dom is at the back of the class, calling out good mornings to everyone, throwing silly challenges on the table and basically flicking everybody's personalities on like lights in a dark hallway.

We've been friends ever since.

You're reading this book because you're looking for something more. Before I wrote this forward I carefully read this book too. Dom and I have spent hours together, talking business, hanging out, strategizing and laughing.

I've heard the deep backstories of some of the stories and case studies you're going to read here. He's walked me through exactly how he starts with nothing and builds multimillion-dollar companies from scratch.

When I say from scratch—I mean from nothing. He doesn't even get bank financing, or lean on family for loans. He builds his own companies from a simple spreadsheet to success—smiling and laughing all the way. He's incredibly focussed and motivated. He works really smart.

And then I see him helping others. What you see in Dom is a construction business coach. I just see Dom as any any-business coach. I've seen him at work.

Remember that gym I talked about? Dom got to talking with the owners when they were doing less than 300,000 a year. He's coached them to well over $1 M. Not only that, he has stood with them as their coach and mentor as they spun off and sold other companies. They're now the largest, most profitable gym in their network, with a huge community of monthly members.

Not only have I watched him do it for himself and others, but I've also had him come in to work with my team at my construction maintenance company. He showed my team the same things you'll read about here—and I used Dom's systems and tools to get that company up to 2M in sales in under 18 months. I then sold that company, following the plan Dom laid out with me.

If you want to learn how to be a construction millionaire I really don't think you could find a better guide than Dom. This book really matters. If you listen to Dom's podcast you'll understand how he brings a different perspective to the table. He talks about things business owners crave talking about.

The problem is we, as owners and leaders, have nobody to talk to. We can't have these types of conversations with our Foreman, our Book keeper or anyone on our staff—they just don't get it.

And we can't have these conversations with our father-in-law or even a good friend—if they're not in business, and if they're not success-minded, they just won't understand how many things we have to juggle in our minds at once.

That's why these construction millionaire secrets are so important. This stuff doesn't get taught in school. And for most of us, these secrets weren't shared at dinner, over our kitchen tables either.

You have to learn them by being around other people who are using them. You have to watch and observe people's attitudes to success and the motivation they have for winning.

You and I have never met. I don't know you—but I know something about you. You want more. You're proud of the work you do and what you stand for, and you're ready for a bigger challenge.

This book will lay out the steps you need to get there. I'm living proof that Dom's coaching works and I know that it will work for you too.

Martin Hunter

President, Urgeo

INTRODUCTION

Welcome to Construction Millionaire Secrets. This book has been written in grey hair and wrinkles—and not just mine!

In these pages, you'll hear the stories and find out exactly *how* other construction business owners—just like you—have started from humble beginnings and grown multimillion-dollar companies.

The truth is you don't need a lot of time (or a business degree) to build a million-dollar construction business, you just need **Simple Systems**. Those systems are usually kept secret, but once you see them, here, you won't be able to unsee them.

I help contractors build million-dollar construction businesses even if they're not sure where to start—and I do that by showing them how to use those Simple Systems.

Simple Systems are the key.

Let me ask you . . .

Do you want to grow your construction business, but find yourself scattered, frazzled, and pulled in 100 directions from

1

the minute you get up until the minute you flop into bed, only to do it all again the next day?

The Simple Systems you'll learn in this book are the secrets of other construction millionaires.

And all of these people came from humble beginnings. Most don't have a diploma. They started when their families were young and money was tight. In many cases, they were new immigrants with very little command of English.

Let me share with you what I showed them.

I'm Dominic Rubino and I'm a businessman just like you. For the last 20 years, I've been able to start, build, run, and eventually sell 2 of my own companies.

It all happened because of what I learned. I had to learn how to work smart, not just hard.

But this isn't just my story, it's the story of other construction contractors and how I showed them how to become construction millionaires.

You probably already know this, but waking up earlier, working harder, and doing everything yourself just isn't the long-term answer.

The truth is, **you don't need a fancy college education**. And you don't even need more time in the day to have a successful business that runs without headaches.

Working hard might have gotten you where you are now, but you can probably already tell it's not going to get you to where you want to go next.

Don't waste any more time. This guide is a shortcut that will solve the frustration and fuzziness you're trying to look through.

After 20 years of working directly with construction and contracting business owners—whether it's a family business, a couple of partners, or YOU, alone against the world—this is the best, tightest, cleanest method I've ever put together to help you:

- get the results you want,
- learn how to use Simple Systems, and
- build a team that will help you get there.

This works because it's proven.

Hang on—let me prep you for these secrets.

Do what I did when I first learned this stuff: slow down. Take your time. These are big ideas. Let them sink in. Enjoy the process.

WHO THIS BOOK IS FOR

The secrets shared in this book aren't restricted to any type of contractor or type of construction work. This book is about building business people, not tradespeople.

If you're driven to succeed and you do great work, and people love working with and for you, then this book is for you.

Here are examples of the people who have benefited from these secrets.

Contractors: If you're a contractor or subcontractor who wants to build your business and have more control over your life and money, this book will help you do that.

General Contractors and Builders: If you're building projects where you have lots of other sub trades working with you, you're going to love this book. You'll quickly be able to recognize who the strongest subs and trades are—and who's not going to make the cut.

Residential Trades Professionals: Residential tradespeople have so much flexibility because the residential homeowner has less time than ever before, less DIY skill than ever before, and more access to cash than ever before. You're going to love this book.

Service Work: If you do service work, you already have a leg up on other trades who do a project and move on. In this book, you'll hear me talk about Recurring Revenue, which is the lifeblood of a service work company. This book will accelerate your journey to success because you're already using the big gears to your advantage.

Commercial and Industrial contractors: There is big money to be made (and lost) in large commercial and industrial projects. The better your company is at using consistent systems and processes, the more the big GCs and PMs will enjoy working with you. You'll definitely get massive takeaways from this book.

Family Business: A family business is a delicate dance that I'm very familiar with. If you're part of a family business, this book has big pieces in it that will help you guide and grow and change direction the way you need to in your company. Feel free to reach out to me if you have private questions. This book will give you exactly the kind of information your family needs to get beyond wherever you're feeling stuck.

The solo business owner: If you are the sole business owner running a crew and working at building a business you're going to love this book. It will show you exactly how other solo business owners have done it. You'll find the shortcuts, the tips, the tricks, the hacks, the workarounds, and everything you need to build this business the way you want it to be.

Partner business: If you have a business partner, both of you should read this book. You'll have so many ideas for how to work better as partners and use the advantage you built into your company from the beginning—the advantage of having 2 people to split the heavy load that solo business owners carry alone.

New Immigrants: If you're a new immigrant, this book is exactly what you need. Things might seem tough for you at times, but please remember: at some point all of us were immigrants to this country. It was the immigrants who came before you—who chose to work smart and work hard—that built the country to what it is today. Now, we need you to take us into the future. This book is going to give you a huge boost.

WHAT IS A CONSTRUCTION MILLIONAIRE?

I got a phone call. A father-and-son team had been listening to my podcast and wanted to learn more about how I do what I do. Let's call them Paul and Riley.

When I set the appointment, I made a huge mistake: I forgot to make sure that all of the partners would be on the phone.

When the appointment time came, it was just me and the son, Riley. Paul the father, couldn't make the call.

Paul and Riley run a great company, and they've made a great name in their local market.

After a couple of questions, I started to see their first challenge—they didn't see themselves as business people.

They get a job and pour heart and soul into completing that job. They do great work, but as soon as that job is completed, they have nothing until the next contract rolls across their desk.

Nothing.

On top of that, I quickly learned that their marketing was 100% based on referrals and word of mouth. That meant that they never knew when another deal was going to land. It was the exact definition of feast or famine.

Riley was taking the call from his work van parked outside a Dunkin' Donuts.

As Riley started into his coffee, I asked him what he and his dad had been doing to change things in the company.

"Well", he said, "Paul thinks everything is fine".

"Riley", I asked him, "*is* everything fine?"

"Uhhh, no", he said. "Paul thinks that as long as we're busy, things are good. And we can only produce so much work, so he's okay with a bit of time off between jobs".

I could tell that Riley had a lot on his mind, so I concentrated on taking notes.

Riley continued. "Dom, I love working with my dad. He's just got a different way of doing things".

"Riley", I said, "can we come at this from a different direction? What do you want out of this business?"

There was a bit of a silence. I think this might have been the first time he'd been able to ask himself that.

"Uhhh, well, I was kind of hoping this business would be more than we have now. My son is about 3 now and it puts a lot of stress on my wife and I being so tight with money all the time. I just know our business is good and that we do good work so how come Paul and I are barely pulling out anything?"

"Bingo", I thought to myself. Now Riley has his frustrations on the table.

- He wants more.
- He knows he can do more.
- They do great work he's proud of.
- He and his partner have different ideas on what growth looks like.
- They've gotten as big as they can and feel stuck.

I can work with that.

The homework I gave Riley was to get himself and Paul back on the phone with me. I had to leave it there—they *both* had to want this.

I'm not here to force success on anybody or tell them what the definition of success is.

But I do know that 2 of them were trying to provide for their families with a business that does under $300,000 a year.

Those guys were barely pulling out a wage.

They're exactly the kind of guys who could turn their business into a million- or multimillion-dollar business by taking the right steps, asking themselves the right questions, finding shortcuts, and not wasting time and energy trying to reinvent the wheel all by themselves.

The fact is, people need construction trades now more than ever.

There has never been a better time to be in business. The demand is high, wealthy clients have money to spend, and they have less time to play around with DIY projects.

That means you and your construction company can pretty much shoot fish in a barrel.

Take Riley and Paul, for instance. They're already doing $300,000 a year as a construction company. As a matter of fact, they're the perfect $300,000 a year business.

With a few smart changes, they could build that into a $600,000 a year business if they really wanted to. You'll see lots of people on my website who have doubled the size of their business.

And once you have a $600,000 a year business that's working nicely, it's easy to turn that into a $1.2 million business. Every $1.2 million business is running on Simple Systems. What's next, you ask? Well, by now, most people have figured out a few of the secrets you'll learn in this book—but they're usually doing things in the wrong order or inconsistently or they've forgotten the things that let them grow in the first place.

If you want to be a Construction Millionaire or multi-Millionaire, you simply have to ask yourself the question: now that I have a $1.2 million business, how do I turn that into a $2.4 million business?

By working for so many years with so many successful people, I've realized that the questions stay the same but the *answers* change as a company grows. The limitation of most business owners is the same limitation Frank has right now.

Paul thinks everything is fine as long as he's busy. Paul is happy to just **work hard**.

But that's the old way of thinking. Riley is happy to work hard but he also wants to work *smart*. Riley sees the opportunity. Paul just sees the next job on the next job site.

We'll talk about this later, but so far, we're still talking about revenues, not profit. And by profit, I mean cash in your jeans.

Think about the biggest, most successful multimillion-dollar construction contractor in your city. How did they start? Where I live, the 4 biggest construction contractors all started as framers or general construction companies. And now they build high-rise towers and redevelop suburbs.

They started in the '80s. Just to help you remember the '80s, that's when movies like *Top Gun, Karate Kid, The Breakfast Club*, and *Full Metal Jacket* came out. Or, if it's more your style, you might remember *Fast Times at Ridgemont High* and *Cheech and Chong!*

Look, in just 40 years they went from driving a pickup truck and living in a nice bungalow, to being multi-millionaires employing thousands of people and taking home millions of dollars in *profits*.

You might think they've been touched by a magic wand or that they made a deal with the devil.

Nope. Sorry, it's nothing as crazy as that. They just went and learned the secrets.

The goal of this book is to share what I have learned about what works (and what doesn't) from companies like that.

Before we dive in, you might be wondering why everyone doesn't know these secrets.

To answer that, just look at our school system.

How can you have underpaid teachers—making $50,000 a year—training young minds to think like millionaires?

Even at the college and university level, where professors are making $80,000 a year, those are professors who are really good at being *professors*.

If going to school was the guaranteed ticket to business success, every professor would drive a Lamborghini, and every elementary school teacher would drive a Tesla.

Instead, our school system trains people to be good *employees*. It doesn't train people to be good leaders or business owners.

It trains people to memorize instead of being creative.

It trains people to pass or fail instead of trying again, trying another way, doing it differently, coming up with your own solution, and making it work no matter what.

It forces people to sit and learn, when maybe standing and doing is the best way for them to learn new things.

And teachers stop kids from asking too many questions, when questions are the building blocks of wisdom.

No wonder this book had to be called Construction Millionaire *Secrets*.

These ideas, these ways of thinking, can only be learned if you get in with the right crowd of people who are all moving in the same positive direction.

If you're reading this, you're already a rare person—you're asking questions and looking for answers.

Let's do this. But first . . .

WHO THE HECK IS DOMINIC RUBINO (AND WHY SHOULD WE LISTEN TO HIM)?

As a professional business coach, it's my job to hide in the wings. The only people who know about me are other business owners and entrepreneurs.

And I have my own Millionaire Secrets as well.

When I was in corporate, I ran a multimillion-dollar division.

Later, I built and sold a number of companies in various industries, including construction trades.

I hope you can tell that I like to have fun, so I'll share the names of 2 of my trades companies:

- *The Yo-Ho-Ho Light Co.*—I started this business in high school. I installed Christmas lights, just my buddy Dean and I in my '83 Toyota Mirage!

- *Ladder-Man! Home Services*—This is 1 of the 2 painting companies I've built.

When I first started my own companies, I failed quite a few times before things kicked in.

It was when I put myself through formal training as a business coach that things changed for me.

I found a mentor who was a millionaire many times over. I knew I was onto something. It was from him that I added WORK SMARTER, to my parents' lessons of working HARDER.

It was from him that I learned the systems, the processes, the checklists, and the flowcharts of success.

I wish the story was more exciting than that, but success in business comes down to having Simple Systems and a handful of rules (and following those rules every day in every situation).

In 2000, I became a certified business coach and I did very well.

Doing "very well" as a business coach is measured by just 1 thing: are your clients getting the success they want? My clients were making more money and taking more time off than they'd ever been able to before.

At the end of my first year of coaching, the head office in Australia reviewed my coaching scores and asked me to be an international trainer. There were only 7 of us in the world.

So, I flew all over the world training other executives on how to use their business background and start their own consulting company as a business coach.

At the same time, I was also working very hard at reinventing a small side-business I had started years before, when I was working in the corporate world.

It was just a fun side business I did on evenings and weekends. I sold used junk on eBay—and when I say junk, I mean *junk*.

The most popular things I sold were old LED calculators and video game consoles (Atari, ColecoVision, Intellivision, etc.).

But that little business had a huge problem: I was running it sloppily. I didn't have systems for inventory, for running ads, for getting back to customers, or for processing payments. I was running it out of a garage and you could tell.

So, of course, I turned my attention to this little side business. If business coaching was working for my clients, why wouldn't it work for me?

After putting systems in place, I realized that my first problem was really a supply problem. So I sat down to make a plan, just like the Construction Millionaire Secrets I'll share with you in this book.

That's how I reinvented that junk company and turned it into an online bookseller.

A few months later, I branched out and turned it into a mail-order pharmaceutical company. When I eventually sold that business, my annual sales were $120 million per year.

I retired at the age of 38. My wife and I flew to Italy to celebrate and spent 2 weeks biking through Tuscany.

Riding through the beautiful hills, I kept thinking (and laughing)—how does a guy like me, with no business degree, start a mail-order pharmacy, build it to $120M in sales and then sell it?

It just proves again that you and I don't need a degree to build a million-dollar (or multi-million dollar) business. I found my mentor and dove in. He showed me the Simple Systems and a handful of rules

Anyhow, being 38, I got bored with retirement.

So, I became business partners with a very famous business author named Brian Tracy. I had originally met him and Robert Kiyosaki when I was training other business coaches.

Brian wanted to start a business coaching franchise using the material he was teaching from stages all over the world. I'll bet some of you (or your parents) bought cassettes and CDs from Brian at some point!

When I bought the global franchising rights from Brian, we had 6 franchisees. Six.

When I sold that company, I had grown it to over 230 locations around the world.

You know why I sold that company? Because I was traveling way too much. My family needed me and I was sick of traveling 2 weeks out of every month.

Later in this book, I'll share this reminder:

If you stand for nothing, you'll fall for anything.

I learned that from wise people and I know it's true because I tested it again and again.

Ok, Dom, So where does working with construction business owners fit in?

Good question. All I've ever had in the industry was 2 painting companies and a small home reno company. I've never owned a company like yours.

I'm in the business _of business._ I'm not the tools guy. I'm not here to make you a better contractor. I'm here to show you **how to be a better business person who _happens to be_ a contractor**.

I'm not here to make you a better contractor.
I'm here to show you how to be a better businessperson
who happens to be a contractor.

That's why this works—just like why dentists don't pull their own teeth.

Anyhow, a big part of being a successful business coach is public speaking.

I've been speaking for different trade associations at conferences, trade shows, and board meetings since the early 2000s.

I like working with construction business owners because talking to them is the same kind of conversation I grew up with at my kitchen table and family get-togethers.

Your typical white-collar business owner talks a lot but doesn't move very fast. A blue-collar business owner makes a decision to do something and pretty much does it. I like that.

Professional contractors are also quick to call BS if they see it. I like that because I can call BS on them as well—and they don't get offended. Try that if you're the business coach of an insurance company or law firm!

My public speaking led to the creation of 2 different construction industry podcasts. I'll tell you more about them at the end of the book—right now we need to stay focused.

Let's dive in, and help you become a Construction Millionaire.

CHAPTER 1

BLUEPRINTS FOR SUCCESS

MILLIONAIRE?

This book and this curiosity you have about how to change your business into a well-oiled million-dollar machine is about working from the neck up.

The real change that will create a million- (or multi-million) dollar business is in who you become when you start to walk, talk, act, think, and grow like a million-dollar business owner.

Because being a millionaire starts in your head.

Speaking of which, let's get something straight: if you're truly committed to building a successful construction business, we need to start at the very beginning—and that includes what we mean by *a million dollars* in the first place.

Be clear. Do you want a million dollars in *revenue* or a million dollars in *profits*?

I can get you to both of these milestones, but as you can probably guess, it takes a little longer to get to a million in profits than it does to get to a million in revenue.

We throw around that million-dollar number a lot, but as you've probably already found out, getting to a million in revenue is a big deal.

If you've already done it, congratulations. But keep reading—you'll still get value from this book because I'll show you how to make your next million and the next million after that.

If you're still working on making your first million, this book has everything you need to get there.

One of my first clients told me

*"Getting to my first million was tough–
but the next million was easier."*

MINDSET

Let's put this million dollars in perspective—that way, as you go through this book, the steps you need to take will be a lot clearer to you.

Your mindset is 1 of the most important places to start thinking like a million-dollar construction business owner.

Some logic:

Did you know that it only takes $83,333/month to have a million-dollar business?

If you want to work 5 days a week, 50 weeks a year, then you're looking at a 250-day working-year.

So that means your company only needs to produce $4,000 of work per day.

And that's only **$500 per hour, 8 hours a day, every day for a 250-day year**.

Now, just to look at it from a different point of view, let's change our logic for a second.

Instead of talking about *working days per year*, let's talk about how many jobs it would take to invoice $1 million in one year

Divide your average job size by a million dollars and that will tell you how many jobs you need to complete in a year to be a million-dollar contractor.

Example: If your average job size is $5,000, then you only need 200 jobs a year to hit $1 million.

That's only 16.6 (call it 17) jobs a month.

Obviously, you can't produce all that work on your own, but in this book I'm going to show you how to build a company filled with the right people who can help you get to your goal.

THE "WHO AM I?" SECRET

Let's start at the very beginning. We can't build anything successfully without first being clear and honest about who we are. Think of it as a blueprint. Would you build something important without a set of plans?

We need to get your plans out of your head and onto paper. They have to come to life!

So, to build a million-dollar construction business, you'll absolutely need to master your thinking first.

Back in my corporate days, I worked in an oil and ranching town. My ranch buddies had a favorite saying:

"If you stand for nothing, you'll fall for anything."

STORY TIME

Before we get started, let me tell you a story and ask a quick question.

You go for a beer with 2 of your buddies. They see your success in business and ask you for help.

Since you're a busy and successful contractor dealing with high-ticket jobs, you don't have a lot of time to waste—so you want to help the friend who can use your advice the most.

You want to help someone who is *motivated to take action* on the advice you'll give him.

So, you ask both of them the simple but powerful coaching question, *"why?"*

"Why do you want my help?"

Your first buddy, Frank, says, "I wanna make more money".

So you ask him "Why?" and he tells you he wants to buy nice stuff—like a newer truck and a bigger ski boat.

"Good answer!" you think to yourself.

But you decide to ask Frank 1 more time, *"Why* do you want to make more money?"

Frank just looks at you and says, "Because. I. Want. More. Money! Duh".

Now you turn to your 2nd buddy, Stan, and ask him the same question.

"Stan, why do you want my help?"

Stan says, "Well, I wanna make more money too".

"Of course you do", you think to yourself.

So, you ask Stan, *"Why* do you want to make more money?"

Stan says, "I have some things I want to take care of".

"Hmmm", you think. That's a bit of a vague answer.

You ask, "What kinds of things?"

Stan goes on to tell you that his mom is in an old age home. Up until now, Stan has only been able to afford a shared room for her. So, she shares her room with 3 other ladies, each of them separated by a simple curtain.

One of the ladies in the room has dementia. Because of that, she's up all night long, yelling and screaming, talking to herself. Stan's mom simply can't get any rest—or peace and quiet.

Stan finishes by saying "I want to make more money so I can afford to put my mom in a private room. She took care of me my whole life. She deserves this".

You've now heard the **why** from both of your close buddies. **Which of them do you know will do *absolutely anything* to reach his goal?**

That's the kind of *why* I'm asking you to figure out with me now.

By the way, this isn't a cute business coaching story I tell to prove my point. That's a real story I heard, years ago, from a business owner.

Second-Buddy Stan is a real guy. I showed Stan the secrets and his mom is doing much better now.

Nothing drives us like the love of family.

So let's figure out:

- who you are, and
- what you stand for!

This will also tell us who you *aren't* and what you *won't* put up with, because if you stand for nothing, you'll fall for anything.

Construction Millionaires already know this very well!

WHO AM I?

List 3 things **you've done** that make you proud.

List 3 things **other people** do that make you disappointed.

Based on these 2 lists, how would you describe yourself? This is **Box A.**

(Example: I'm a family guy. I started this company from nothing. I'm a really good electrician, and my clients trust me.)

List your strongest skills **as a tradesperson** in order of priority.

> *(Example: Strong electrical skills, good problem solver, I have the best equipment, I'm good at math and mechanical skills.)*

List your strongest skills **as a business person** in order of priority.

> *(Example: People trust me. I'm honest. I get the job done.)*

List the kinds of things **you see other contractors** do that frustrate or disappoint you.

> *(Example: Overcharging customers, not showing up, installing the wrong equipment. Using the wrong tool for the job.)*

Based on these 3 lists how would you describe yourself as a construction contractor? This is **Box B**.

> *(Example: I'm a good electrician people can trust.)*

Take **Box A** and **Box B** and combine them into 1 sentence that describes who you are as a person and a contractor.

Who am I? I am . . .

> *(Example: A proud electrician who has the skills, knowledge and personality to help my customers when they need me most.)*

To download this worksheet, go to:

www.constructionmillionairesecrets.com/bonus

Congratulations! You now **have the start** of your company culture, written out. I'll show you how to bring this to life in Chapter 4, where we'll talk about your team.

WHAT IS MY WHY?

This seems like such an easy question, but it is the biggest driver of your success in growing a million-dollar construction business.

"Why?"

That's the question: WHY? Just like we asked Stan and Frank in the story above.

Fill in the following boxes so that we can figure out your *why*.

This is an important exercise because it will drive you in your darkest hour, on your longest day when you feel like the world is against you.

I learned an important lesson from a good friend many years ago. He said,

"None of us are in business for business reasons, we're all in business for personal reasons."

Makes sense, right? If you just wanted to make money, you could go and get a job. But you want something more. That's why you invested in yourself and invested in this book.

So, **what's your *why*?** Fill in this worksheet to get it out of your head and on paper.

Why did you decide to open a **construction business of your own?**

> *(Example: I always wanted to go out on my own. I was doing so much side work that I knew I could make it. Plus, I didn't really get along with my old boss, so I just took a chance and got started.)*

Why did you decide **not to get a job** (or keep the job you have/had)?

> *(Example: I was so busy with side work and I was turning it down. But I made a lot more on my own, so I knew I could do it.)*

How do you **define "success"** for yourself in this business?

> *(Example: I want to take care of my wife and kids. I work crazy hours now and I can't keep going at this pace. But I also want to take home more money.)*

What is **the feeling you want** to have when you reach success?

> *(Example: I want it all to be calm. I want it to be predictable. I want less problems.)*

Who is **relying on you** to succeed?

> *(Example: My wife and kids. I also have 2 guys working for me.)*

Who is **watching you and learning** how they need to live their life?

> *(Example: My kids. My daughter is 7 and my son is 3.)*

What do you want them to say when they think back on **the impact you've had** on them?

> *(Example: My dad took care of us. He had his own company but he still came to all our games and practices. We took nice vacations and he gave me a good life.)*

How would it make you **feel** if you failed?

(Example: I can't fail.)

Using the answers you've given above, please fill in this box. What is your *WHY*?

(Example: I'm here to run this company so I can take care of my family and show them what success and independence looks like. I'm here to show them what winning looks like.)

To download and print this exercise, go to:

www.constructionmillionairesecrets.com/bonus

At this point, I have often found that people start talking about family, about their kids, and about how they want something *more* for their kids.

STORY TIME

Back when I was living in the oil town, I had a client named JD. He was about as straight a shooter as you were ever going to find. He was a construction engineer for oilfield exploration. Starting from zero, he had built his company to 80 people. Oil money is stupid money and his revenues were just under $100 million.

JD always came across as so casual, but he was laser-focused. We never really talked about family, we just talked business.

But I remember when his son had run into some trouble in college and was moving back home.

JD had that slow, cowboy way of talking, filled with confidence and determination. He said something to me that keeps popping into my head—it might be 1 of the best how-to-be-a-dad quotes I've ever heard.

"My son watches me to see the man he needs to become, and my daughter watches me to judge the man she'll choose in her life. I gotta figure out where maybe I showed him wrong."

Think about what motivates you.

SECRET #1: You need to understand your *why*.

Congratulations! You're learning the Construction Millionaire Secrets.

You've just completed an exercise that only the most senior, experienced, successful entrepreneurs in the world will ever do.

Keep the answer in the box called "What is your *why?*" in a private place. You'll need it when we talk about your team and goals.

This will also tell us who you aren't and what you won't put up with.

You're now ready to move onto the next Construction Millionaire Secret.

THE CRAZY NUMBER THAT CHANGES EVERYTHING

I'm about to talk to you about your own personal time management. So, in the next few paragraphs, you might be surprised to be learning about a number.

Think of this as a millionaire contractor's PPE. It's your hard hat, your vest, and your steel-toe boots. Knowing and thinking about this number will protect you from making the wrong decisions.

The number is your **Revenue Responsibility per hour (RR/h).**

This is 1 of the deepest and most closely held secrets to being a Construction Millionaire.

The only place you'd ever get a hint that this number even existed is if you watch *Shark Tank* or *Dragons' Den** and listen very carefully to what the panel of entrepreneur investors are talking about.

A Construction Millionaire understands his or her Revenue Responsibility per hour (RR/h).

To understand yours, we need to calculate it twice. I'll show you why.

First calculation: Our actual RR/h

Here is the formula to calculate your RR/h:

SALES / HOURS WORKED

For the first calculation, take last year's total sales for the year and divide it by the number of hours you worked in the business last year.

For example, let's say your total sales last year was $500,000. Let's also say you worked 6 days a week, 50 weeks a year, for a total of 300 days. Multiply that by 10 hours per day. That equals 3,000 hours of work per year.

LAST YEAR'S SALES ($500,000) / NUMBER OF HOURS YOU WORKED (3,000) = $167 PER HOUR

So, what this first calculation tells us is that your Revenue Responsibility as the owner was $167/hour last year. This is your current RR/h.

No, that doesn't mean you're going to charge your work out at $167 per hour! What that means is that your company is responsible for producing $167 per hour of product or services.

Of course, use your own numbers so this calculation makes more sense.

Now, here's the ***secret inside the secret***—because you can't open this lock until you first figure out where the door is.

Second calculation

We're going to calculate your RR/h a 2nd time.

But this time, we're going to do it as if you are already a Construction Millionaire!

Use the same formula.

SALES / HOURS WORKED

I also want you to stretch yourself and set a new, more realistic target for the number of hours you work a year. For this example, let's assume you still work 10-hour days but *only* 5 days a week.

I'm giving you permission to take weekends off. Because, in this book, I'm also going to show you how to work smarter, not just harder

Now, your goal is to work 5 days a week, 50 weeks a year, 10 hours a day, for a total of 2,500 hours worked in a year (*Please feel free to change this number to suit your situation!*).

Here's your new RR/h:

$$\$1,000,000 \text{ / } 2,500 = \$400/\text{H.}$$

Are you freaking out right now?

See, this is 1 of the biggest Construction Millionaire secrets.

SECRET #2: If you want to be a Construction Millionaire, you have to start thinking, acting, planning, and goal-setting as if your RR/h is $400 per hour.

It's a big leap and that's why people ignore it.

So, does this mean that you have to bill out your time at $400 an hour?

No.

Does this mean you have to manage the company and your people so that you produce $400 per hour in billable work?

Yes.

To download a simple worksheet to calculate your RR/h or share it with a partner, go to:

www.constructionmillionairesecrets.com/bonus

How does my RR/h impact my time management?

As you read this book and start to learn the other secrets, I want you to be very aware of how you're using your time.

If a salesperson calls just to chat for half an hour, he had better be adding value to your company to the tune of $200 for that 30 minutes. If not, you have my permission to hang up.

If you have a problem employee who's causing drama and grief for the rest of your team, you can finally put a dollar number on how much company time they're wasting.

I've seen it before. "Disruptive Dave" says or does something every week to annoy or frustrate the rest of your crew.

Of course, the people on your crew come and talk to you about it, eating up 15 minutes here and 30 minutes there. Before you know it, your whole day is gone and all you've dealt with is shrapnel from Disruptive Dave.

Or he shows up late, or drunk, and starts blaming traffic, the weather, and parking for why he couldn't show up on time. But since he's really good on the tools, you give him another chance, and another, and another.

What's the real cost to the company? Well, for each of the hours you, as the owner, have spent dealing with Disruptive Dave and the chaos he leaves behind him, he's costing your million-dollar construction business $400 per hour.

It's time to let Disruptive Dave go, even if he's the best pipefitter, welder, cabinet maker, carpenter, drywaller, painter, tile setter, bookkeeper, or forklift driver in the world. He just costs too much.

A Construction Millionaire would let Disruptive Dave go and use that wasted time to find a better employee with a better attitude.

(*) Shark Tank (USA) and Dragons Den (Canada) are both TV shows where multi-millionaire investors hear business proposals from start-ups looking for money to fund their company.

Shark Tank airs in USA, Mexico, Vietnam, Australia, Israel

Dragons Den airs in Canada, New Zealand and most of Europe

Tigers of Money is the original, from Japan

CHAPTER 2

FOUNDATIONS

Now that we have the blueprints for success behind us, we can concentrate on building strong foundations for your million-dollar construction business.

I've often had construction business owners secretly whisper to me,

*"Dom, I don't know what I'm doing . . .
I didn't go to business school."*

No problem.

I've been a professional business coach for 20 years, and I've been building and growing my own companies for 25.

Most of the successful entrepreneurs I know and have had the pleasure to work with either didn't finish high school or, if they went to college, are now doing something completely different than what their degree is in.

YOUR 2-FINGER MBA

You don't need an MBA (Masters of Business Administration) to be successful in business. But, if you think you really need one, I'll give you **your 2-finger MBA** right now.

Hold up your index finger and the one next to it—you know, the one you use for sign language when you're driving! Look at those 2 fingers. One is taller than the other, right? Here's your 2-finger MBA:

Point to the longer finger and say, "Keep my sales high".

Point to the short finger and say, "Keep my expenses low".

Congratulations! You have a 2-finger MBA.

Want your own signed and certified 2-finger MBA to hang on your wall? Download the certificate at **www.constructionmillionairesecrets.com/bonus**

That's all you need to understand to be successful in business. We don't have to overcomplicate things.

If you look around your local market at the biggest, most successful construction companies, I bet you'll find immigrants who came to the country 20, 30, 40, or 50 years ago. In a lot of cases, they didn't even speak English when they got here.

And look at them now.

"It's not what you got, it's what you do with what you've got."

Even though I had a chance to go to school, I guess I'm in the same boat. I went to university and got a BA in archaeology. I know—*WTF? Archaeology!?*

Yes, and I never did a day of work in that field.

I worked in the corporate world for a few years, but I absolutely hated it. I always knew I wanted to have my own business

When I left the corporate world to start my own business I knew that I needed my own foundations to finally be successful.

What surprised me was that 1 of the biggest secrets I learned in corporate was also 1 of the biggest secrets I learned in starting my own multimillion-dollar companies.

THE IMPORTANCE OF SIMPLE SYSTEMS

Here's your next Construction Millionaire Secret,

SECRET #3: Keep. It. Simple.

When I say "keep it simple", I'm talking about the wise insight you get from your favorite uncle or successful friend.

"Simple systems build successful companies."

We're going to talk a lot about **Simple Systems** in the rest of this book.

Brutally honest, factual, elegant, *simple* systems.

You probably already use simple machines every day—and you know how powerful they can be.

Simple Systems are the machines we use to build a business.

All Six Simple Machines

Let's take a look at the secret systems other Construction Millionaires are using right now.

Simple Systems to make better use of your time

We all get 24 hours in a day—and I want to use mine better than the next guy.

When it comes to living the life I want, how I choose to use my time is where it all starts.

If you're not using a calendar to schedule your meetings and daily to-do lists, you have to get started on that *today*. I want you to start living by your calendar.

SOLUTION → If you do nothing else, find a way to get *insane* about managing your time. It does not have to be on a laptop or on your cell phone.

Sometimes people say, *"But Dom, you don't understand what it's like. I can't create a schedule. Things come at me all day and I have to deal with them"*.

BS.

Yes, things come at you all day AND you have to choose when and how you'll deal with them. If you want to get in control of your time, **you** have to control *what* you do *when*.

If you're running a company, your first priority is running the business.

SOLUTION → Go online and print out a "week at a glance" blank calendar. Now write in all of the things that need to happen in your week.

For instance, here are some daily time blocks:

7:00 AM—Start work
7:30 AM—Site walkthrough
2:30 PM—Leave job site
3:00 PM—Paperwork, quotes, estimates
5:30 PM—Be home

Now add blocks of time for things like:

- client meetings,
- payroll,
- site inspections, etc.

Every time you say to yourself, *"I can't do it. Somebody else controls my schedule"*, I want you to change that thought.

What you need to say to yourself is, *"How can I make it so that I get that task done but do it on my time and terms?"*

Simple Systems for communication and accountability

If you feel like your crew is holding you back, let me ask if you are communicating:

- enough?
- properly?
- clearly?

Look, I'm not asking you to have more meetings. I'm asking you to have shorter, better ones.

I'm asking you to be clear in what you want done, and to follow up with your crew on what you've asked for.

Use your favorite sports team as an example. If they're on a losing streak, is it really just the players?

Imagine that you had to step in and help the GM and president fix your favorite sports team, only to find out they:

- had no team meetings, and
- no one was tracking things like:

    - contracts,
    - practices,
    - workouts,
    - meals,
    - shots on net,
    - penalties, or
    - scores.

Then you also find out they don't:

- watch game tapes,
- study their competition,
- run set plays, or
- have audibles they call.

What would you think? What would any armchair quarter-back say?

SOLUTION → Understand that, as the leader of the company, it's your job to manage people and have those people complete the job. As a leader, you have more responsibility than anyone else.

Your crew is there to work the tools. *You* are there to **manage people and tools to get the job done.**

That's why I introduced you to the RR/h formula. That's the kind of logic that runs through the mind of a Construction Millionaire.

Simple Systems to make a plan, stick to the plan, work the plan

This is 1 of the secrets you came here to find. In my last company, I was partnered with a very well-known author and business consultant named Brian Tracy.

One of his quotes that I always liked goes like this,

_____

"Opportunity knocks more often than people think,
but it shows up wearing work clothes
and that scares them."

_____

The work I'm talking about here is the kind you do from the neck up. I want you to start to think and plan before you do. It's a different kind of work than being on the tools.

SECRET #4: Make a strategic plan,
stick to it, and follow it.

Even if you've never done one before, It's easy to put together.

**SOLUTION → Just sit down with some blank paper
and plan out your goals for the next year. Then
break it back down into what you want to get done
in the next 3 months. And then break it down again
into what has to happen this week.**

My 1 year goals

My 3 month goals

Goals this week

Today

Then put those things in your calendar and *get them done.*

Boom. You now have the world's best and easiest business plan. Stick to it. You'll get there.

The Simple System for creating and building your company culture

Almost 100% of the time when I talk about this one, business owners give me a funny look. They think I'm talking about unicorns and rainbows.

I'm talking about what you and your company stand for—your *values.*

Your eyes might already be glazing over, but follow me for a second, OK? This is how millionaires think about things.

Values are the rules you have for living. Some of the common ones I've heard over the years are Family, Faith, and Fitness (health).

On the business side, I hear values like Work Smart, Proud of Our Work, and Profit.

Remember that if the owner hasn't told their crew what the rules are for being on the team, they're leaving their crew to make them up.

What is the worst thing that could happen if you told your crew that you expect them to be Proud of their Work?

How about the business value of Profit? Some of us don't like to talk about money with our crew. OK, fair enough, but ask them to work for a week without pay, and see how important money is to them.

When I'm upfront and honest with my crew that we are here to:

- Work Smart,
- be Proud of Our Work, and
- Make a Profit,

I open up the conversation about what that means to me and to us.

LOOK AT THINGS FROM A DIFFERENT POINT OF VIEW

That brings us to the next Construction Millionaire Secret.

SECRET #5: You have to look at the playing field differently than everyone else.

We're going to go up to 30,000 ft. and look down at the company. I want you to see your business operations as if they were a flowchart.

Successful business owners work really hard at keeping things simple, clear, and easy to understand. Simplicity is your friend.

So let's look at your company as the simplest picture we can make it. This will let you see all the moving pieces and also where the gaps and opportunities are.

This flowchart is your playing field.

CHAPTER 3

MILLIONAIRE MATH

This chapter will change your life. It changed mine.
This info is the backbone for *how* I've been able to:

- show others how to build million-dollar companies (and become millionaires),
- buy companies,
- sell companies,
- analyze my marketing, and
- find out where a company is "sick" and then know exactly what to do next,
- get their life back,
- re-invent their business while it's running,
- take care of aging parents,
- buy kids braces, put them in travel sports, and pay for college,
- drive a newer truck, towing a bigger boat, to a nicer cottage on a prettier lake, and

- show their father-in-law they have what it takes (yup—
  I've heard that a few times now!).

Before I knew what you're about to read, I stumbled, fell, and
failed in my own companies. Don't get me wrong—I did great
work, but I barely pulled a wage out. It sucked.

Then, after I "got this", here are some of my results:

- I've employed 1,000s of people.
- I've coached 100s of companies over 20 years and shown
  them how easy it is to get into the millions.
- I've spent more time at home as Dad, husband, and son
  than I ever would have.
- I started, built up, *and eventually sold* 2, large, multi-
  national, multi-million-dollar companies of my own.

On top of that, I get the honor of talking to the smartest, nic-
est people in the world who always want to know the same
things.

1. What's the secret to working smarter, not just harder?
2. How can I really build this business and get it as big as I
   want it to get?

Let me tell you that when I first learned this secret, I had to
slow down and make sure I got it right.

I knew I was seeing something important.

There's a little bit of math in this. And, if you're not a math
person, you might try to skip this chapter. I'm not a math

person and I knew I had to slow down and walk through it step-by-step.

Let's get into it.

LESSONS FROM DOUG'S KITCHEN

There are 3 basic business formulas that you already know. The secret is in knowing when to use these 3 formulas and how to weld them together.

SECRET #6: Know the Customer Formula, Revenue Formula, and Profit Formula, when to use them, and how to use them together.

I didn't learn this stuff at my kitchen table as a kid. As an adult, I took courses. I read books. And then, when I got trained as a professional business coach, I finally got it. That was back in the year 2000.

My mentor was an Australian multi-millionaire who finally laid it out for me in a simple, easy to understand format. I had finally found out the secret.

Before we get into this secret, let me ask you: What did you talk about at *your* kitchen table as a kid?

I only thought about that kitchen table conversation after something really simple happened.

In my group of friends, I'm the guy with the trailer. You might be that guy (or gal), too. So, every once in a while I get a call from a friend who needs my trailer.

Of course, since they don't have anything to tow it with, that request usually comes with me and my truck too!

STORY TIME

There I am, on Saturday morning, at my buddy Doug's house. Doug is a great guy and probably 1 of the best businessmen I've ever met.

As we're having coffee, his son, Sam, comes in and starts talking about his hockey fundraiser. They're selling Krispy Kreme donuts in front of the grocery store.

Friday night sales didn't go so well and his son is bummed out.

Doug asks him, "Why do you think sales were slow?"

Sam: I think it's our location. It kind of sucks and we're stuck there and we can't move.

Doug: But you had people coming by?

Sam: Yeah we had lots, but they're already going in to buy groceries and they don't want donuts.

Doug: So, you don't have a problem with leads, you're just having a problem making the sale?

Sam: Uhh, I mean, yeah, I guess.

Doug: So, really, all you guys have to do is figure out how to get those leads to buy from you, right?

Sam: Ya, I guess.

Doug: Tell me what you're saying to people as they walk past you.

Sam: We say "Hi". They know we have donuts, Dad—they can see them.

Doug: Did *anybody* buy from you?

Sam: Ya, I guess. We sold about 10 boxes, but they're gonna give us 40 today! (He's bummed.)

Doug: What did you say to the people who actually bought from you and what did you say to the people who didn't buy?

Sam: Well, if we had a longer conversation they would buy from us.

Doug: So, your sales are based on conversations, not the amount of people walking by because you have lots of those right?

Sam: Ya.

Doug: What did you say to people to get them into a conversation?

Sam: We talked about hockey. Lots of people used to play too.

Doug: People who used to play hockey would buy from you more often?

Sam: Ya, I guess.

Doug: Sam, I think if you want to make more sales, you've got enough people walking by. You just need to figure out how to start a conversation. Once you have a conversation, you get the sale. And people who used to play hockey are more likely to buy from you. So, today, when people walk by ask them if they ever played hockey. Don't ask them if they want to buy donuts.

Sam: Ok, I guess . . .

Now, I'd *like* to tell you that this chat went perfectly and Sam was taking notes and looking up at his dad as if he was the smartest man in the world. Nope.

Sam is a great kid, but he's still an 11-year-old.

But as I was listening and watching this normal conversation at Doug's house, I realized that Sam was growing up learning—in his own kitchen—how to take apart a problem and attack it piece-by-piece using a proven formula.

Look, I'm the luckiest guy in the world. I grew up with a great family and loving parents who taught me about work ethic and standing behind my word. I'm sure Sam is learning that too.

But there's no way they would have taken that problem apart the way Doug did.

My parents would have told me to work harder, and maybe stay a little later. They would have even offered to drive me to the store so I could start a bit earlier. Oh, and smile more.

Sound familiar? All of my parents' love, guidance, and suggestions at my kitchen table were to remind me to work *harder*.

Doug showed his son how to work *smarter*.

Do you see the difference? Sam is already learning secrets most kids will never learn. How he uses those secrets is up to him.

Doug's story? Years ago, he left a big corporate job and bought a small, struggling manufacturing plant.

It was kind of tripping along and Doug knew he could fix it. When he bought it, sales were around 750k a year. 12 years later, Doug sold that company for $43 million.

?????!!!!!

I'm going to show you the steps Doug and I take when we reinvent a company from the inside out.

THE 3 FORMULAS SECRET

This is so easy you might skip past it. These 3 formulas, used together, are a Construction Millionaire Secret:

1. The Customer Formula.
2. The Revenue Formula.
3. The Profit Formula.

When I sit down behind closed doors with a business owner who wants to grow, it's very common that they say:

- *Dom, I don't know why, but we just don't seem to have enough* **customers.**
- *Dom, things are pretty good, but we seem to be stuck at X in sales (***revenue***).*
- *Dom, we're selling and we're always busy, so how come we're not* **profitable?**

You probably already know these formulas, but it's how we *use* them that matters. I want to show you how to weld those 3 formulas together—because these 3 formulas are the blueprint for reinventing your business.

This is 100% a Construction Millionaire Secret. If you ask 1 million business owners if they know this secret, *maybe 10* will say yes.

But, if you sit down behind closed doors in a meeting with the top 10 largest and most profitable construction companies in your city, *all* 10 of them will know these formulas.

If you like to watch *Shark Tank* or *Dragons' Den* on TV, you can hear these formulas come to life when the panel asks questions to the startup companies that are pitching business ideas and investment opportunities.

One more thing to inspire you to learn this: in the example that follows, you'll see how a $750k/year company grows to $1,089,000. And then, just for fun, I'll show you how to get it to $5 million in 5 years.

Where would you be now if you learned these secrets 5 or 15 years ago?

The Customer Formula

This is the formula that Doug was talking about when Sam was having trouble selling donuts for his hockey fundraiser.

LEADS × CONVERSION RATE = CUSTOMERS

Nice and simple.

Let's break the formula apart. And just to have fun with this, let's say that your construction specialty is building playgrounds on the moon.

Remember, it doesn't matter what business or industry you're in, **what matters is how you analyze the business and take action.**

This formula will work whether you sell hot dogs, run a muffler shop, own a bakery, or you do mega-million federal infrastructure construction projects.

This will work whether you do service contracts in HVAC,

build fences, fix roofs, build and maintain pools, paint houses, fix drywall, or build scaffolding for the rocket launches at NASA!

Play with your own numbers. Download it at:

www.constructionmillionairesecrets.com/bonus

Leads: Count and keep track of the number of people who are interested in having a conversation with you about "building playgrounds on the moon".

Conversion Rate: This is just like measuring your batting average. It's an important number because it tells you how good you are at turning your *leads* into *customers*. You can really only calculate this after you know how many leads you've got and how many customers you have.

This was Sam's issue when he said "we're talking to lots of people but we're not making sales".

Customers: This is a lead who has signed an agreement and made full payment to you. This might sound funny, but it's important to be very clear on this definition—a customer is somebody who has *paid you.*

The Revenue Formula

Now that we have a clear understanding of how customers come into the business, we want to understand how those customers turn into money.

CUSTOMERS × AVERAGE SALES SIZE × AVERAGE NUMBER OF TRANSACTIONS PER YEAR = REVENUE

Let's break that down.

Customers: A customer is somebody who has paid you.

Average sale size: This is simply the sale price of your average job.

Average number of transactions per year: All you do here is count how many times a customer makes a payment to you over the year. If you build playgrounds on the moon, then this number is probably 1.

That means that when a customer signs a contract with you, you do 1 deal with them a year. (We'll get to this later, but if you also sell them a monthly maintenance agreement, you have 12 MORE transactions a year.)

When we multiply customers by our average sale size and then by the number of transactions we do in a year that gives us our *revenue*.

So . . .

1. If I have 1 customer who bought a playground on the moon, and
2. they paid $50,000 for the contract, then
3. my total sales for the year is 1 × 50,000 = $50,000.

Revenue: also known as total sales for the year or "top line". In Australia and New Zealand, you call this "*turnover*".

The Profit Formula

Now, let's define the Profit Formula. It's actually a 2-part formula because we need to calculate **gross profit** and **net profit**.

$$REVENUE - COGS = GROSS\ PROFIT -$$
$$OPERATING\ EXPENSES = NET\ PROFIT$$

Get the Excel version here:

www.constructionmillionairesecrets.com/bonus

Revenue: Total sales for the year.

COGS: Cost of goods sold. The most basic definition is materials and labor. Sometimes this is called "cost of sales". (By the way, if we were really building playgrounds on the moon, the transportation costs are coming up in operating expenses.)

Gross profit: This is just the profit left over after you pay for materials and labor. This is not the money you take home because we still have other expenses to deal with.

Operating expenses: People sometimes call this OPEX. These costs include rent, equipment, inventory costs, marketing, payroll, and insurance (and moon transportation).

Net profit: This is also called "bottom line", or net earnings. This is just a measure of what's left over after EVERYTHING else has been paid. This is where the bonus money comes out for the owner.

The secret-within-the-secret is that **how you lay this out on paper really impacts how you take action.** But I had to give you the definitions before we lay it out.

The first thing I want to point out is that, as you look at this all laid out, **you can't do anything after the equal sign**—that's just the outcome. But, you have complete flexibility on anything *before* the equal sign.

Here's what I mean.

When I first sit down to look at a company on paper with the owner, they'll tell me where their frustration is.

For example, they might say, "Dom, how can we get more customers?"

Okay, that's a good question, but it's the *wrong* question. Because getting customers is an *output* and we can't control the output until we control the input.

My old business partner, author and business management guru Brian Tracy, used to remind his audiences that *"thinking is the most important work we can do"*.

As business owners, we have to think of the right question to ask for each business problem.

The Simple System that Construction Millionaires use is to fall back on this formula. The formula holds the questions.

If the problem is "not enough customers" then the question is both:

- How do I get more and better leads?
- How do I increase my conversion rate so that my leads turn into customers?

Remember the formula:

LEADS × CONVERSION RATE = CUSTOMERS.

So, I only get more customers when I attract more leads and sell them a work contract.

THE CONSTRUCTION MILLIONAIRE FORMULA

Let's dig into the secret-within-a-secret: it's how you lay out the page.

I know—how could it be so simple, right? I wish I had the answer but I think it has to do with the way humans see patterns.

Here's how you write the entire formula. It doesn't have to be fancy, it can be hand-drawn on the back of a napkin, it's super easy to make in Excel, or you could print and fill it at:

www.constructionmillionairesecrets.com/bonus

I like doing it on paper. Then I can really get into it.

C	D	E	F	G
	Last 12 months	% Change	Next 12 Mos	
Number of Leads				Customer Formula
X				
Conversion Rate %				
=				
Number of Customers				Revenue Formula
X				
Average Sale				
X				
Ave # Sales Per Period				
=				
Revenue				Gross Profit Formula
-				
COGS				
=				
Gross Profit				Net Profit Formula
-				
Operating Expenses				
=				
Net Profit				

In column D, labeled "Last 12 Months", all you have to do is go ahead and write in your actual results.

It's important to be brutally honest with yourself here. I'm going to show you how to become a Construction Millionaire *inside* this formula so you can see what you need to do to get there.

Now look at column E. In this column, we're going to look at how much change we can introduce to this part of the business in the next 12 months. That will change the number in column F.

C	D	E	F
	Last 12 months	% Change	Next 12 Mos
Number of Leads	48	10%	53

So, in this business of building playgrounds on the moon, you went back and looked at your files and saw that you had 48 interested people call your company over the last year. So, we put the number 48 in column D.

Then we asked ourselves, how much do we think we could increase our number of leads in the next 12 months? Do I think it's possible to increase my number of leads by 10%? What would that take? How do I get leads now? If I got a little smarter or used some different tactics would I be able to get 10% more leads than I had in the last 12 months?

If you think you can do 10% better, just do that math. 48 + 10% = 53 (It's 52.8, but I just rounded up).

Is that doable? It doesn't sound that hard. If you agree, then put the number 53 in column F.

I find that a lot of people rely on referrals and word-of-mouth in the construction industry. That equals 2 strategies. Let's add online marketing in there. Do you think you could get another 4.8 leads next year by adding online marketing?

In my work as a business coach, I have **72 different strategies** just for lead generation that my clients can choose from—so it doesn't matter what you're currently doing, there are always more opportunities available. With the right approach you can add 10% more leads in a year.

Now let's look at conversion rate.

In most cases, a business owner won't know their conversion rate. That's because this formula is a new secret. Thankfully, it's easy to work it out backwards!

This business owner already knows their number of customers last year—it was 15. So, when we figure out 15 / 48 we find out that our conversion rate is a little over 31%.

We're making great progress and we already have 3 rows started! This is what it looks like so far.

C	D	E	F	G
	Last 12 Mos.	% Change	Next 12 mos.	
Number of Leads	48	10%	53	
X				Customer Formula
Conversion Rate %	31%			
=				
Number of Customers	15			

Again, let's apply our Simple System. We know we can't do anything after the equal sign, so I can't magically say I want 10% more customers.

But *I can* challenge myself to increase my conversion rate by 10%. Remember, conversion rate is just the batting average. If you close 3 out of 10 deals now, what would it take to increase that by 10%? Do you think you could increase it to 34%?

Sure you can. Especially if you focus on getting more of the right customers. That row shouldn't even worry you because there are 38 different strategies that can be applied to increase the conversion rate in a business.

See, this isn't magic, it's just a formula. The simple secret that Construction Millionaires use is to reduce everything to its simplest form—again, keep it simple—and focus all of their energy on fixing the right thing at the right time.

In this next picture, look at how that has increased the number of customers this playground installation business has done.

C	D	E	F	G
	Last 12 Mos.	% Change	Next 12 mos.	
Number of Leads	48	10%	53	
X				
Conversion Rate %	31%	10%	34%	Customer Formula
=				
Number of Customers	15		18	

I have to point out that it's important to ask if your company *can* make the jump from 15 to 18 clients. If not, there are some business operating or people systems we need to fix first (more on that later).

But that's why we asked the question! Go fix it if you need to.

At this point, we've just finished building the Customer Formula for your business. But a Construction Millionaire knows there are 2 more formulas to look at.

Now for the Revenue Formula.

Earlier in this chapter, I told you that a playground on the moon cost $50,000. So that will go in the row called **average sale**. Now I'll ask the business owner if he or she thinks they can increase that job price by 10% in the next year.

Usually, the answer is "yes". In this case, that's an additional $5,000. Most of us in construction have a product or service that we believe is the best solution for a customer but they often don't buy it. And usually that add-on solution is about 10% of the sale price already.

So if all we have to do is get really good at learning how to sell that extra $5,000 product as an add-on, we've already increased our average dollar sale in the next year.

The next thing the formula asks for is for us to calculate our average number of sales for the year. Again, for most construction companies this is 1 (one).

In the next chapter, I'll share another Construction Millionaire secret that outlines why and how you need to find a way to increase this number.

But what if you found a way to make 1 additional sale to 1 out of 10 customers in the next year. Could you do it?

Hey, maybe not. If you're a framing contractor that might be tough—once a building is framed, it's framed. If you have a situation like that, it's even more important that you start to view yourself as a business person, not a trade contractor—otherwise you'll spend your whole life fooling yourself that things just have to be this way. They don't.

We just need to build your business in a different way so that you can increase the number of transactions a different way. More on that later!

Here Is what your Construction Millionaire Formula will look like and how it will impact your top-line revenue.

	C	D	E	F	G
		Last 12 Mos.	% Change	Next 12 mos.	
Number of Leads		48	10%	53	Customer Formula
X					
Conversion Rate %		31%	10%	34%	
=					
Number of Customers		15		18	Revenue Formula
X					
Average Sale		$50,000	10%	$55,000	
X					
Ave # Sales Per Year		1		1.1	
=					
Revenue		$750,000		$1,089,000	

Boom. Just like that, you can see the steps that you need to take for this business to grow from $750k to being a million-dollar business.

The secret is in the compounding effect. Because we're applying small changes to a number of places, we're getting a bigger impact.

Be very, very careful if a salesperson calls your office and wants to sell you a new lead generation program. That's fine if you have a system for converting those leads into customers, but if your system and process for how you *sell* is broken, all you're going to do is waste money stuffing good leads into a bad process.

At the same time, you might be in a position where you can't increase your average dollar sale for different market reasons. For instance, you might be a garage door dealer and the manufacturer dictates your pricing.

I'd like to call BS on that, but until you and I discuss it, let's let it be.

Just for fun, let me show you what happens to this playground-on-the-moon installation business after 5 years of trying to get 10% better each year in the areas of:

- lead generation,
- conversion rate,
- increasing sale prices, and
- increasing number of transactions per customer in a year.

This is how a $750k/year business becomes an "overnight sensation".

	Last 12 Mos.	% Change	Next 12 mos. Yr 1	Yr 2	Yr 3	Yr 4	Yr 5	
Number of Leads	48	10%	53	58	64	71	78	
X								
Conversion Rate %	31%	10%	34%	37%	41%	45%	50%	Customer Formula
=								
Number of Customers	15		18	22	26	32	39	
X								
Average Sale	$50,000	10%	$55,000	$60,500	$66,550	$73,205	$80,526	
X								Revenue Formula
Ave # Sales Per Year	1		1.1	1.2	1.3	1.5	1.6	
=								
Revenue	$750,000		$1,089,000	$1,596,176	$2,336,962	$3,421,546	$5,009,485	

You can call BS on this if you want, but only after you sit down and do the math yourself.

Look at how this company is now $5 million a year. The owner is probably taking out $500k.

In year 5, they only have 39 customers. That's only 3.25 installs a month.

Pick this apart all you want. Please do, because, in doing so, you'll start to sit down and work through the formula step-by-step. That's exactly what I want you to do.

Hang on—what if you're suck? What if all you can do in the next 5 years is get this business to $2.5 million in revenue? Is that really a failure? According to a BusinessKnowHow.com survey, only 7 % of all the businesses in the USA have sales over $1 million.

So, if you hit *half* of your goal, you would be in the top 7% of all business owners in the United States. I'd be pretty comfortable to assume the same trend in numbers for Canada, Australia, New Zealand, and Europe.

Let's do the Profit Formula next.

This is probably a great time to remind you that I'm not a math guy. When I first learned this part, it freaked me out.

I registered to take a business coaching course in another city. I knew I had to meet this Australian multi-millionaire and learn his system for re-inventing a business while it was still running.

So, I shut down my office, kissed my wife goodbye, and got on a plane. I wasn't going to know anyone else in that training room, but I had been looking for this information my whole life.

Every night after class, while everyone else went to the hotel bar, I went up to my hotel room. I sat down and drew this formula out by hand.

My head was spinning. Why had I failed? Did I shut down my other companies too early? What had I done wrong?? How could I have done things differently to keep those companies alive?

So, I entered my old numbers in column D. I used my past failed businesses for all of those questions. I used my Christmas light installation company. I used my painting company. I used my handyman service company. I worked through the formula sitting on the floor. I just kept running the numbers.

How had I missed this?

I just sat down and played with the formula. It stung. I could see where I'd messed up. Up until then, I'd only learned how to work hard. And now I could see how to work smart(er).

Putting it all together

I call revenue the big lie.

And I hear this lie a lot, usually when I'm out with my wife's friends. I get cornered in the kitchen by some loud-mouth guy who's the husband of some lady I don't like.

And he starts talking *at* me and bragging, asking me what my revenues are. "What's your top line, Dom?" and "What do you figure you'll sell this year, Dom?"

Then, of course, he'll tell me that the company he works for is going to do $300 million in revenue this year. And his division is going to contribute more than it ever has because he's so smart.

There I am, stuck in the corner between the fridge and the sink, praying for Diedre to come by and rescue me.

Quietly, the voice in my head is saying, "Buddy, I dont give a flea's fart what your revenue is. Who cares? I'm not here for revenue. I'm here for profits."

But I keep smiling, because I'm a good husband and this guy will never get it.

Business owners have it all on the line, every day.

OK, let's look at profits. We're going to keep building out the formula.

Our revenue last year was $750,000.

Our COGS (Cost of Goods Sold) is 65%.

So, our gross profit is $750,000 – 65% = $262,500.

Now we have to subtract our operating expenses. For this business, the operating expenses are 27%.

So you multiply your revenue by 27% = $202,500.

And that leaves you with a net profit of $60,000.

Remember, all we've done so far is take a picture of our current situation. It should look like this:

C	D	E % Change	F
	Last 12 Mos.		Next 12 mos. Yr 1
Number of Leads	48	10%	53
X			
Conversion Rate %	31%	10%	34%
=			
Number of Customers	15		18
x			
Average Sale	$50,000	10%	$55,000
x			
Ave # Sales Per Year	1		1.1
=			
Revenue	$750,000		$1,089,000
-			
COGS	65% << 487,500 >>		
=			
Gross Profit	$262,500 <<Revenue- COGS>>		
-			
Operating Expenses	27% <<Revenue * 27%>> 202,500		
=			
Net Profit	$60,000		

I love this stuff. Remember, if you're not a math person and you find yourself getting flustered, slow down and maybe even take a quick break but come right back and pick this apart piece-by-piece.

I am not a math guy and I can dance the tango inside this thing, but it took practice!

THE PROFIT FORECAST

We need to do our forecast because the exercise of doing that will give us the actions we need to take in the company.

If you're doing this while sitting in the corner at Starbucks, you're going to look like a crazy person muttering to yourself. So be it. At least nobody will try to take your chair.

The only thing different in this profit section is that we're looking for ways to *reduce* our expenses. In every category above this, we were trying to increase things by 10%, but now we're going to try and reduce things by 10%.

In my 1-on-1 work with business owners, I have a running list of 81 different ways to reduce cost of goods sold (COGS) and 74 different ways to reduce operating expenses.

Think of those as tools in my toolkit.

Those tools give us the flexibility to challenge ourselves and find a way to reduce both of those categories by 10% in a year.

Can you think of a way to reduce your COGS by 10% in the next 12 months? Think of ideas like buying in bulk, negotiating better deals with your suppliers, finding ways to reduce your labor overheads, etc. In the case of our playgrounds-on-the-moon company, our goal is to take our 65% COGS and reduce it by 10%. That works out to a new COGS of 58.5%.

As a Construction Millionaire, you'll also sit down and think about ways to reduce your operating expenses by 10%. So, instead of 27% operating expenses, your company's goal is to get that down to 24.3% for the year. You can do that by rethinking the way you do the work that you do.

Here are just 4 from my list of 74 different tactics.

A Sample of 4 out of 74 Ways to Reduce Operating Expenses

1. Use technology better.
2. Outsource some of the work your company does, especially office work.
3. Look for subcontractors to take some of the work away from you at a lower rate than you can deliver it.
4. Really tighten up your cash flow situation by having solid systems in place for accounts receivable and accounts payable. There is a lot of meat on that bone!

This is what the impact will be on your business after **just 1 year of knowing exactly** which levers to push, which levers to pull, and which ones to ignore.

C	D	% Change	F
	Last 12 Mos.		Next 12 mos. Yr 1
Number of Leads	48	10%	53
X			
Conversion Rate %	31%	10%	34%
=			
Number of Customers	15		18
x			
Average Sale	$50,000	10%	$55,000
x			
Ave # Sales Per Year	1		1.1
=			
Revenue	$750,000		$1,089,000
-			
COGS	65% << 487,500 >>		58.5% << 637,065 >>
=			
Gross Profit	$262,500 <<Revenue- COGS>>		$451,935
-			
Operating Expenses	27% <<Revenue * 27%>> 202,500		24.3% 264,627
=			
Net Profit	$60,000		$187,308

I hope you're starting to see the pattern here. The important part isn't having all the answers, it's **having the right questions**.

A Construction Millionaire knows how to pick this formula apart inside and out.

Congratulations, you now have 1 of the biggest, most impactful secrets at your disposal.

Now let's talk about another Construction Millionaire secret.

RECURRING REVENUE

This secret is why banks, insurance companies, Dunkin' Donuts, and Starbucks are so profitable.

It's because they have predictable monthly income from the people they do business with.

SECRET #7: Get recurring revenue.

With banks and insurance companies, we pay premiums and service fees.

Dunkin' and Starbucks have convinced us to use prepaid cards. That pulls us back into the store where they can track our purchases and frequency. Somewhere in the world, your information and mine is on a global-mega-coffee-corp spreadsheet very similar to the 1 we just built together!

Let's talk about money—we could all use more of it, right? It doesn't matter whether we're in business for personal or professional reasons, we should all be thinking about the future of our companies, and that future depends on *money*.

One day, down the line, you might decide to sell your business. How will that look? What if there are a couple similar businesses for sale in your area—will yours stand out?

You can go after (and win) the biggest contracts, but—as this global pandemic made obvious—you might still find the future of your business in danger one day. The solution? **Recurring revenue.** (Some people call it repeat revenue or contract revenue or service contracts.)

It doesn't matter what we call it, what we're talking about is finding a way for your business to be organized so that money comes in regularly. Recurring revenue is nice and dependable. It generally isn't exciting, but it trickles in steadily.

Recurring revenue becomes extra important in times like these—when most contract work froze, we saw that rent, service contracts, and other forms of recurring revenue kept coming into those businesses that had them set up.

It's also important when you go to *sell* your business. All things being equal, a buyer is going to prefer a company with plenty of recurring revenue, because recurring revenue means cash flow, and that's what the smart buyer is looking for.

So how do you get it?

Service contracts

My favorite strategy to increase recurring revenue is service contracts. A $300 maintenance contract might not sound that exciting at first, but consider that $300 a month is $3,600 a year.

If you get 10 of those contracts, that's $36,000 a year. If you get 50, it's $180,000.

The type of service contract you can offer depends, of course, on your industry. For some industries (like landscaping) it's obvious. Others (like pool installation) aren't so clear.

Without spending too much time on this, let me just say that whatever your industry is, **we can find you service contracts**. Trust me. If you don't believe me, give me a call and we'll hammer it out.

The go-to example I like to use is priority on-call service. Depending on your industry, chances are good that there's a market for this—hotels and restaurant chains, for example, NEED service when they need it.

You charge, say, $300 a month for that priority service, but remember that they're not going to call you every month. Maybe they'll call every 3 months, but that recurring revenue comes in all the same.

STORY TIME

Jake runs a hardscaping business. That means he does the kind of landscaping where he builds retaining walls and paved walkways. It's also called landscape construction.

He desperately wanted to find a way for his son to join him in the business, but Jake was also sick of the up-and-down nature of job-by-job contracts.

I challenged him with a powerful question:

> *"Are you a contractor with a couple of guys or are you a businessman who happens to be a contractor?"*

That got him thinking.

So, he started sending out side letters when he submitted a bid for hardscaping.

His first lawn maintenance contract was a museum for $2,000 a month. His son is now running the lawn maintenance division. A few more side-letters and they jumped to $6,000 per month pretty quickly and they will be over $2 million a year in a few months.

That's guaranteed work and guaranteed cash flow in a brand new company.

I showed Jake how to build his son his own division.

How can you do that in your business?

The first time you go out to do 1 of these service visits, it's probably going to feel like a waste of time. Each service contract is just a little trickle of recurring revenue, but as you collect more of them, that trickle becomes a stream.

Rent out

And service contracts aren't the only way to build recurring revenue streams. Real estate is another popular approach. Instead of renting, why not buy your building and charge rent to other tenants?

Have you ever thought of renting your unused or quiet equipment to other crews? It's a great way to get recurring revenue from machinery you've already got. Why let a front-end loader sit around 4 days a week when you could be making money from it?

Thinking outside the box—outside of your contracts—is the key to getting steady streams of recurring revenue.

They might not seem like much on their own, but as you look for and implement new ideas, you'll soon find yourself with steady cash flow that'll take the edge off of challenging markets and increase the value of your business.

CHAPTER 4

TEAM

I hope that when we did the revenue responsibility per hour exercise you recognized that you can't do this alone.

Remember, if you want to be a Construction Millionaire, you have at least a $400 RR/h.

STORY TIME

Chuck and his father-in-law, Tony, started a light commercial construction and tenant improvement company.

Tony was old school, and they did great work, but they would bounce between $900k and $1.3 million in sales in their best year.

Chuck was the Site Super/Foreman and PM, while Tony did estimates and billing.

When Tony passed away, Chuck moved into the office. Apparently it was already a bad year and now he had to hire a Site Super/PM. Stressful times.

He had young kids at home, and didn't really know the estimating and office work side.

As he tells me, at home, his yard was a mess. They had a big tree that needed to be cut back, but the thing was huge and tough to get at. He said there was also a big overgrown hedge.

Since he never got to it, his wife got fed up and called a guy to do it. Chuck tells me he was super pissed—especially because it cost him $750 (yes, this was a few years ago).

"Dom", he told me,

_____

*"that was probably the best 750 bucks I ever spent.
My wife and I got in a big fight but she was right.
I was bidding on a job for $80k and we ended up
winning it. That was a huge job for us. I wasn't going
to win it if I was trimming the $%^& hedge."*

_____

As he grew, he went from doing small retail buildouts to tract warehouses. Most of his work now comes from the Transit Authority and a big phone company campus. His crew pretty much does everything there.

Chuck and I have worked together a few times over the years. He works with me, then takes a break. Then we work together again.

The first time we met, Chuck went from $1.5M to $2M. So he lifted his RR/h from $600/hr to $800.

A few years later he was still around $2M and we went to

$3M. That's a RR/h of $1200. We focused a lot on profitability, not revenue.

Add another break of a few years and now Chuck is $10M/year. He's raised his RR/h to $4,000.

Don't freak out. Chuck isn't carrying that whole load himself. He's doing better jobs, with better margins, and has a tighter team.

He's a long way from getting on a ladder to cut his own hedges. He can't afford to. And, as he reminded me, he can't afford to fall either!

Is that blowing your mind?

This is a Construction Millionaire Secret because **the people that know this number don't talk about it**. And the owner struggling to hit $200-300k/year thinks I'm full of BS.

It's not BS. That number is a flag. A beacon. A reminder. A goal.

When Chuck sits down for a meeting with me, we talk about that number.

We know that this 1-hour meeting has to add value to the company to hit a *minimum* of $4,000/h.

We're making wise decisions and taking action. People are accountable. Goals have time limits.

I've seen Chuck make decisions differently. He hires, manages, and delegates differently.

He runs his company like a team, and we can't afford to waste time.

The result?

The office runs with very little drama—everyone knows what they're there to do. His crew is always working on continuous improvement. Systems are in place and his team follows them.

What do you see looking in from the outside? Nothing. These guys are low key. Boring-looking. Chuck drives a 10-year-old Silverado. He just bought a used quad for the kids.

But what's really going on? In the last few years, while I've been sitting at the table, he has also:

- bought multiple houses that he rents out,
- bought his building and subs out 2 other units and parking,
- bought an additional 20,000 sq. ft. of land, now in rezoning so he can build warehouses,
- kept staff turnover extremely low,

He still works 2,500ish hours a year (10-hour days, 5 days a week), but takes his vacations in Mexico, Hawaii, and North Carolina

Your RR/h is a constant reminder to focus on the most important things first—to do the things that will have the greatest impact on the company, and to do them as quickly and efficiently as possible.

Recently, Chuck bought another company. Even when the deal first hit the table, the team knew it had to have the potential to invest time in.

That small division already has yearly sales that put it in the top 10% of all "normal" companies in their state. The plan is to grow it like Chuck's GC company.

Believe in your RR/h. It might be painful at first, but it will be your friend in the long run.

Uhh, Dom, I thought this Chapter was about "Team".
Doesn't that mean HR and hiring and my people?

Yes, you're right. In order to be a Construction Millionaire, you're going to need to build a finely tuned, smooth-running team. Like Chuck did.

Your team *has to help* you hit your RR/h.

If your team (or someone on it) wastes your time, there's a cost to that. If they can't keep you at this RR/h, or your goal RR/h, **they have to go.**

Once you know the secrets, it isn't that hard. Actually, it's a lot harder doing it *wrong* than it is doing it right!

Here are **4 Construction Millionaire Secrets for team building** you need to know. You'll see that I've laid them out as Simple Systems for you.

1. Hire them right.
2. Train them right.
3. Lead them right.
4. Create and use Simple Systems.

Let me explain.

HIRE THEM RIGHT

In order to run a successful construction business, you can't just hire the first person that shows up.

Yes! I understand that in a lot of places, the labor market is very tight right now.

And it's easy to think "I'll just hire a warm body to throw at the problem".

Except that some of those warm bodies become an even bigger problem than the 1 you're trying to solve with production.

If you had to choose between 3 things when hiring somebody, would you choose skills, knowledge, or attitude?

SECRET #8: Always choose attitude first.

We can train technical skills. That's why there are books on how to build, fix, repair, install, or maintain things.

Attitude is the most important thing.

"I shouldn't have to teach you what you should have learned at your kitchen table growing up."

Here are a few tips, tricks, and shortcuts to figure out if somebody has the right attitude. You might have a few of your own, so use those as well.

If somebody walks up to the job site and asks for a job:

1. Definitely give them a 5-minute interview on the spot.
2. Ask them all the technical questions about your trade that you want.
3. Ask them about their old boss or company
4. If they blame or make excuses about why they're looking for work, take that as a *red flag.*
5. If they talk badly about their last job, *that's a red flag too.*

Now, assuming you like their technical answers, I want you to set up a very simple test—a test to see if they have the right attitude:

6. Tell them you need to think about it.
7. Ask them to **call you back at exactly [choose a time] for the answer.**
8. If they call you back at **exactly** that time, you probably have a winner with the right attitude on your hands. Hire them. You don't have to leave it too long—ask them to call you in exactly 5 or 10 minutes.

If somebody phones the office and asks for a job, have a script on hand for you or whoever answers the phone. Follow steps 1-8 above.

If somebody replies to an online ad for a job posting, reply and get their phone number. Set up a phone call *first* (don't waste time until you know they're worth it). Use the phone script for you or whoever answers the phone. Follow Steps 1-8 above

TRAIN THEM RIGHT

OK, let's hit the secrets to training people right.

Let me start by saying I don't have all the answers. I'm always trying to learn. When I meet a wise person, I gobble up their systems, stories, anecdotes, and observations. Then I combine that with my own experience and use them to improve.

I keep asking wise people, listening, learning, applying, and re-adjusting.

STORY TIME

Harry (Harjit) came to the US from India over 20 years ago.

He's a very nice guy, and pretty soft-spoken and factual. He's also driven. I met him because he owns a number of home trades construction companies in his state. He likes service companies because, *"the clients pay me every month"*.

He and I were both speakers at a conference, and we got talking at the bar after our presentations.

He told me something about training people, in a way I'd never heard it expressed before. He said,

"You either hired the right people and trained them wrong, or you hired the wrong people. Either way, it's all on you."

Did I mention how blunt he is?

> Boom—that's wisdom. He owns more home service franchises than anyone else in the Pacific Northwest. His whole summary of training people is on-point—how my people perform is up to me.
>
> Harry is a Construction Multi-Millionaire.

Ok, how do you train people right?

Let me share a secret observation.

SECRET #9: Construction Millionaires train everybody the same.

It doesn't matter if you have 10 years' experience or you're a fresh high school dropout, everybody gets trained the same.

Training gets broken into 2 parts:

1. Technical training.
2. Culture training—this part involves what it means to be on my team.

Technical training

It will only take you 2 minutes to do this part, but it will pay you back again and again and again for the rest of your life.

On a piece of paper, write down the high points of **your job site expectations.**

Let me start the list for you, and add what you think is important for your crew.

FRED FLINTSTONE CONTRACTING
JOB SITE EXPECTATIONS

1. Getting to work on time (7:15 for a 7:30 start) is 100% your responsibility.
2. Get to our job site by 7:15. Our team is ready to start as soon as the whistle goes.
3. Report to the foreman and get your tools and PPE ready for the day. We work safely.
4. Work starts at exactly 7:30. We take time seriously.
5. Monday, Wednesday, and Friday we have a tailgate meeting that starts immediately at 7:30 at the Muster Station. We work safely, and we get along as a team.
6. Complete the work as discussed with your foreman.
7. Before you report "work completed" to the foreman, ask yourself, "Am I proud of the work I've done?"
8. If not, fix it. We're proud craftsmen.
9. Report completed work to the foreman and get your next assignment.
10. Coffee break is from 10:00 to 10:15.
11. Lunch break is from 12:00 to 1:00.
12. Afternoon coffee break is from 2:00 to 2:15.
13. At 4:45, stop work.
14. Coil hoses, cords, and cables neatly. Bring them to the job site trailer for secure overnight storage.
15. Gather company tools—bring them to the job site trailer for secure overnight storage.
16. Inspect your PPE for safety. We all want to go home safely.
17. Gather your personal tools and meet the foreman at the Muster Station.

To print this list, so you can get started, go to:

www.constructionmillionairesecrets.com/bonus

Is my list perfect? No. I'll bet some parts drove you nuts. Good.
This is your company—make it your own.

When a new hire starts, hand them this list on Day 1.

STORY TIME

Jason has a gutter installation company. He texts that list above to his new hire while they're both standing together. Then he says, "Once you get my text, send me a message back so I know you got it".

Boom—now they can't say, *"You didn't tell me . . ."* and Jason doesn't have to carry paper in his truck.

Next, choose a safety video on YouTube you want your new hires to watch. There are a billion to choose from.

This leads to another Construction Millionaire Secret.

SECRET #10: Find a way to know that your directions are followed.

So, all I want here is to know that I asked them to do something and they did it. Even though you're doing technical training, you're building up your team culture every chance you've got.

Here's the simple system I showed Jason.

At the start of Day 1, he gives the Job Site Expectations I showed you above.

At the end of Day 1, his foreman talks to the new guy. The foreman gives feedback and has a chat about how the day went.

Then, the foreman assigns the new guy **homework that has to be done for the next day**.

The new guy has to watch a YouTube video (Jason uses the ladder safety training video by NAHBTV called *"Safety Toolbox Talks: Ladder Safety"*) and tells him that he'll be asked questions about it the next day.

Of course, the next day, when the new guy shows up and reports to the foreman, we find out if this new guy is going to make it on your team.

A side note: you have to apply this test to everyone for it to have power. You can't have a guy say "F--- this, I ain't watching no video". If he does, let him go on the spot. He just fired himself. He had a shot at being on your team and he blew it.

Culture training

This is 1 of the Construction Millionaire Secrets you're here to learn.

SECRET #11: Create a handful of simple rules, tell your crew what they are, and stick to them like a dog on a bone.

This is actually easier than it sounds, because I'm not talking about the technical rules for doing what you do in your trade. I'm talking about the rules for a high-performing team. Let me give you a few to start with. If you believe in them, steal them from me (and the 20 years worth of other business owners I've worked with) and make them your own. Make these the rules your crew has to follow to join your team and *stay* on your team.

* **Positive**: I speak positively and I look for solutions. Leave the negative talk for negative people.
* **Responsibility**: I know that I'm responsible for everything I do, think, and say. I take that responsibility seriously.
* **Ownership**: I always do my best. I might make a different decision than somebody else but I will stand behind that decision. If you disagree, ask me to explain myself.

Notice that I used the words "I" and "me". Those are powerful words that roll right back to taking responsibility and ownership.

CHAPTER 5

TOOLS

If you want to be a Construction Millionaire, you've got to stop thinking of yourself as a contractor with a crew of guys.

SECRET #12: You need to become a businessperson who happens to run a contracting business, not a contractor with a crew.

My goal in this book is to get you into that mindset.

Construction Millionaires are businesspeople. They know the money isn't just in the sawdust. It's in the Simple Systems that run the business.

My son is 11 years old. He hears me on the phone and kinda knows what I do. But he stumped me the other day by asking, *"Dad, what's a business?"*

I was stumped. It probably freaked him out that I went silent for a few minutes.

I mean, I had to think of a great answer. I want my son to know! What is a business?

Here's what I said:

"A business is just a collection of Simple Systems that helps people solve problems. And the more problems a business solves for people, the better it does."

How's that?

Here are Simple Systems you need to be a Construction Millionaire. We've already talked about how,

- you need to know your RR/h (Secret #1).
- you need a 1-page business flowchart (Secret #5).
- you need to know the Construction Millionaire Formula (Secret #6).

Beyond these, you also need Simple Systems for:

- finding new, great customers (marketing),
- helping the right customers buy from you at premium prices (sales),
- estimating,
- production (what we make, fix, build, demolish, install, maintain, or repair),
- billing and invoicing,
- collections,
- re-sales and referrals,

- managing people, and
- managing the business.

WHO DO YOU WANT TO WORK WITH?

You need to be crystal clear on who gets to be your client.

Who Is My Ideal Client?

Put your phone on silent. Print off a list of all your customers from the last 2 or so years. Go sit at a coffee shop.

The list of old customers should have headings like:

Job Name:

- Address/location
- Job type (*installed a playground for the first School on the Moon*)
- Job source (how did you get introduced to the customer?)
- Job value
- Profitability
- Was it commercial or residential?
- Profit in $
- Profit as a %

Then add these secret headings:

- Hassle Factor (how much of a hassle was this job, location, or customer?)
- Unbilled travel time

Add a notes column:

- Was this job in your sweet spot for skill, and do you have the crew to do these jobs again and again?

STORY TIME

Matt builds high-end custom kitchens. His shop is 45 minutes from 1 of the biggest cities in the US.

The designers in a city 3 hours away absolutely love him. He wins jobs there that look juicy and profitable. But when Matt did this exercise, he realized that although he was building the right kitchens for the right kind of customers, he and his team were driving too much.

Add in tolls, hotels and meals, and expenses creep up quick—remember our operating expenses in Secret #6?

That 3-hour commute each way was actually eating into his profits—and his life.

Once Matt sat down to do this exercise, we realized that all he had to do was develop relationships with designers in his own city. And it turns out that wasn't very hard to do.

The hard part was turning down the work he was getting 3 hours away.

We did it. Matt's sales actually decreased slightly, but his profitability shot through the roof.

Here's a quote from his text message to me.

My text to him: A few weeks ago you told me the impact of coaching on your business in some simple numbers. Sales are the same but profit is up?

Matt:

Sales were actually down about 10% YTD, but profit was up 385%. I'll check the numbers again tomorrow but last year YTD we were showing a loss now it's like 68k or 9% profit.

Sit down and do this exercise. The numbers don't lie–and they are trying to tell you something.

I interviewed Dave Sullivan on my podcast. He's a construction multi-millionaire from the roofing industry.

He discovered the same thing. A Construction Millionaire is crystal clear on "who we are" and "what we do".

For Dave, that meant turning down residential roofs (and windows, doors, dog houses, etc.) and just focusing on commercial maintenance roofing.

For some people, chasing residential work just isn't something they want to do.

Then again, there are people who recognize that residential work has a lot of flexibility and higher profit margins.

Part of your work then is deciding **who you want to work with** and **what kinds of jobs are best** for your business.

Whatever side of the fence you find yourself on, let's talk a little bit about how to get jobs. I'll separate Commercial and Residential work.

COMMERCIAL WORK

Your state, city, province, or country might have specific rules for bidding on commercial work. For instance, you might need to post a bond which you can buy through a bonding agent. Or you might need a contractor's license which can make it difficult, but not impossible.

But if you set your mind and say "I will find a way", you'll find a way.

Let's look at getting commercial work by breaking up the market.

If your company is going to do commercial work, you'll still be doing whatever trade you're in. But in almost every case, you'll be held to a higher standard of completion than on many residential jobs.

Those of you reading this who do HVAC, plumbing, electrical, and fire suppression completely disagree with me right now and that's because you always fall under a special set of permit rules for the work you do!

Usually, when we talk about commercial work, what you're basically telling me is that you want big jobs where you can keep your guys busy for weeks, months, and even years at a time.

Sure, but *why* commercial work?

Things have changed over the last 20 years, but the answer to this question hasn't. I can sum it up in 2 words: **less headaches**.

What that really means is the owner has less headaches in finding new jobs, getting his people to different worksites on different days, and putting systems in place with home-owners for how we get paid for the work we do and what the expectations are for payment.

6 WAYS TO FIND COMMERCIAL WORK

Be a subcontractor

When you look at a huge tower going up in your neighbor-hood and wonder how you can get a piece of that build, the easiest thing for me to tell you is to drive there, walk onto the site, talk to the site super and find out who runs your trade.

Then ask if you can do subcontract work for them. In some cases, they'll say "no". Who cares? Ask again.

Then drive to the next job site and do the same thing all over again.

SECRET #13: There's no one else in this world who can limit your success—only *you*.

When I look at the clients who are now doing millions of dol-lars in the construction trades, I also have to look back at how they started. Colin, Nick, Mark, Farshad, Nico, Vince, Arnell, Doug, Jan, Tyler, Chris, Dustin, Thomas, Jorge, Teanna—all of these companies started off with nothing more than a handful of business cards. And they would walk from job site to job site talking to site supervisors.

In each case, they would just ask

———————

"How can I bid on this job? Or the next one?"

———————

There's no magic to it except hard work and determination.

Work for a general contractor

There are different types of GCs. Find the ones in your city who specialize in large commercial jobs and get on the phone with them. Ask if you can bid on their next project.

Many of them will say "no". Again, who cares?

We are only looking for the "yes".

Imagine if you won the bid to do 1 commercial job—it's worth it!

When you call a large commercial general contractor, they're going to ask what kind of experience your company has in running jobs their size. Price isn't the only factor.

If you're super cheap but you can't complete the job, you're just a waste of their time and energy.

OK, let's do a reality check—look, I'm a positive guy, but I'm also a realist. I'm not going to give you any BS.

Your chance of winning a $1,000,000 commercial contract to do [enter your trade specialty here] is *slim to none* when you first start out.

Why? Because a general contractor won't give you a million-dollar contract until you have proven your experience and skill at producing other million-dollar contracts.

You're going to have to work your way up the ladder. Get your first commercial job at $10,000, then at $25k, then at $50K, etc.

You'll be forced to learn how to produce jobs on budget and on time. You'll learn how to be profitable at different job levels. Heck, you'll even learn what it takes to estimate a million-dollar job!

Something you also may not have considered is the expense you'll have to pay out on a job that size before you even start billing the client.

You have to get your guys on payroll, with benefits, make sure they have PPE, buy the supporting tools and equipment, *and* have the trucks, insurance, and bonding in place.

If you're doing *zero* commercial work now and you get awarded a million-dollar contract tomorrow, your head is going to spin before it falls off!

SECRET #14: Construction Millionaires are wise – they grow slowly and deliberately.

Find property managers

Big buildings and complexes have property managers who look after the ongoing maintenance and repair. There's even an opportunity for you with property managers who look after smaller apartment buildings.

If you want to get commercial work so that you don't have to go meet homeowners and sell them 1 job at a time, then these kinds of property managers are a great option.

The easiest way to find property managers is to:

1. go to Google,
2. type in "property manager + [your city]",
3. print the list, and start calling.

Serious property managers belong to trade associations.

So, wherever you live, you can simply search for "property manager association + [your city]".

Let's use Austin, Texas as an example.

Here's what comes up.

Austin National Association of Residential Property Managers

austin.narpm.org

Austin National **Association** of Residential **Property Managers**®

Austin Apartment Association | Austin, TX – Home

www.austinaptassoc.com

Austin Apartment Association | Austin, TX. Home · About ... AUSTIN APARTMENT ASSOCIATION. SERVING THE RENTAL HOUSING INDUSTRY SINCE 1964 ... Austin, TX. Shippy Property Management. Maintenance Technician. Austin, TX.

BOMA Austin: Home

www.bomaaustin.org

Building Owners and Managers **Association Austin** . . . Finally, the commercial real estate industry has a professional certification that provides . . . and guides the next generation of **property managers** toward greater responsibility and success in . . .

There are even more but I got tired of copy-pasting for you!

Under each of those listings, you're going to find 50-100 different property management companies.

All you have to do is introduce yourself to them, let them know the kind of work you do, and keep following up with them until they send you some work.

Remember, you only need 50 jobs at $20k to be a Construction Millionaire. That's 2 jobs a month.

Can you complete 2 jobs a month at $20k each?

Strata councils, HOAs, and commercial property managers

For this category, it's important to know who they are and what they do so you can understand how you can help them.

When you drive down the street and see an apartment or townhouse complex, you're seeing gold.

You might even live in one of these complexes yourself.

In different cities, states, and provinces these go by different names.

- HOA: homeowners' association.
- Strata Council: A "strata" type of real estate ownership is where you have shared interests with the other owners in the complex. For this discussion, it's the same as an HOA.

The beauty of these types of property management is that they have ongoing work, and once you're their trusted and go-to contractor, they'll probably just call you directly.

Imagine an apartment building with 300 units. If only 2% of the tenants move out every month, that works out to 6 apartment units each month that need repainting. Add onto that common areas and pretty soon you can find yourself quite busy just servicing large apartment complexes.

In the case of painting apartments, it looks like residential work but it's actually a commercial job!

Small commercial property owners

In every city, there are very smart, hard-working people who have saved and put aside their pennies to buy their own real estate portfolio.

They own houses, small shopping centers, small apartment buildings, and even some warehouses.

If you're a reliable tradesperson, they're going to call you when they need work done.

Just because we call them small commercial property owners doesn't mean they're not important.

What's important is that these guys really value their time. They don't have a huge office with lots of people who can manage tradespeople for them, so if you do a good job and can work completely without supervision, they're going to love you.

Okay Dom, sounds great but where do I find these guys?

That's the million-dollar question, and that's why you bought this book—I'm going to give you a Construction Millionaire Secret that no one ever shares.

SECRET #15: You need to be a lion in a room full of zebras.

You've got to think like your perfect client and hang out where they hang out.

These small commercial property owners see themselves as real estate investors, so you need to go where real estate investors go, and meet them there.

It doesn't matter if you meet them online or offline.

One of the biggest real estate investment online chat rooms is called BiggerPockets. You can go into the forums and see their conversations, their questions, and their concerns.

Of course, when somebody brings up an opportunity in your area you can reach out to them and offer to do the work on their property!

The website is **BiggerPockets.com**.

Commercial bid websites

Be careful, because **these can waste a lot of time**.

In every city, state, and province, there are different websites where commercial bids get posted.

It looks fantastic! You'll see hundreds of opportunities to bid on big commercial jobs.

So does everybody else. Bidding on these jobs usually takes you down to the lowest common denominator. Price only.

Choose carefully when answering these bid packages and then go back and reread this chapter from the very top and find your own commercial contractors to do estimates and tenders for.

FINDING RESIDENTIAL WORK

Now for residential work.

If Construction Millionaires have a secret superpower, it's definitely the ability to look at numbers and read reports.

I want to be the first to admit that **I hate looking at a report full of numbers.** The way my mind works, I would much rather see charts and graphs and color.

And that's where we're going to start our search for *more* and *better* residential work.

Heat Maps

Usually, we make the most money when our guys are on the tools, not when they're driving. Each part of your territory has a different impact on profitability.

A **Heat Map** is a marketing tool used to show you where your clients are clustering. It's a simple system that stops you from doing unpaid, unbillable, frustrating, and time-wasting driving around town.

To create a Heat Map, first make a list of all your best jobs from the last 2 years. Plot those addresses and locations on a map. Where those places cluster is your Heat Map. When you work in that zone, you know you're set up to make (and not lose) money.

If you're just starting and you've never had clients, look at your city map and think about where you want to work. Outside that ideal zone is a no man's land.

Look at the following map. In this example, where is the best place for your company to focus?

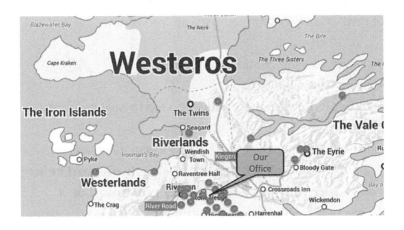

To make your own Heat Map, follow these steps:

1. Ask your administrator to pull a report of the last 2 years' clients.

2. Have them make a chart that looks like this:

Customer (or Job) name	Revenue	Profit in $$	Street Adress	Notes
Smith	30,000	3,000		toll bridges- need to add to Estiamte
Jones	22,000	2,500		
Chan	17,000	1,700		
University Museum	110,000	11,000		brutal site access, drive time
Hospital Utility Room	64,000	6,400		
etc				
etc				

3. Using Google Maps, turn the info on this chart into a map that looks like the Westeros map above.

Getting there, getting around, and getting out

Think about time and access considerations for different parts of town. Can you split your city up into zones?

- Zone 1 would be standard pricing.
- Zone 2 is a bit extra.
- Zone 3 has even more added to keep these jobs profitable.

Note that I'm not saying you have to add more pricing to Zone 2 or 3. What I'm saying is that you need to **think hard before you *reduce your price* to win a job in Zone 2 or 3**.

You're better off to add services and hold to your original estimate, instead of dropping your price to win.

Think about this: How much does it cost you to have 1 technician in 1 vehicle stuck behind a train for 30 minutes? This is a profit leak that Construction Millionaires think about for adding *something* in your internal pricing for commuting.

SECRET #16: Use Heat Maps to find and
price residential work.

Put your Heat Map on the wall, and think about it when you
put a final price together!

TRUST AND THE WEALTHY BUYER
(SALES SKILLS)

Now, more than ever, people will finally be placing value
on things that really matter. In the short and medium-term,
price will be less of a front-facing issue than you've ever had
before.

That's because of our next secret.

SECRET #17: Trust will be the main driving
factor in making buying decisions.

Yes, "price" has always been *a* factor, but people tend to think
that price is the *only* thing that wins the deal.

Wrong.

Price is only 1 of 4 main factors. It's always been this
way. I'll lay this out so that it's easy to follow as a reference
document.

Feel free to share this with anyone else on your team who
sells new contracts and jobs for you.

First, let's set the stage properly.

As a business professional—no matter what type of contractor you are—**you're here to help people buy**. That's how we help.

"Selling is something you do TO somebody and helping people buy is something we do WITH people."

If you're an honest, ethical business person, I'm sure you agree.

And this is why price dropped in importance for buying decisions during the COVID-19 pandemic and will stay in this lower position as we move forward. **Trust is taking over as the primary motivator.**

Here are **the main things that motivate people to buy**. Remember, this list has always been true.

1. Budget
2. Need
3. Timing
4. Trust

Knowing and understanding these 4 motivators and the questions that come with them has always been important, but now they are *critical*.

You absolutely must keep this list in mind in the following places in your company operations:

- Marketing (how you find people interested in what you do),

- Sales (how you help them buy),
- Branding basics (how people see, act, and react to your company),
- Appointment setting (moving quickly towards decision making),
- Sales presentation (learning what the prospect wants, finding solutions, getting agreement),
- Handling objections (clarifying terms of the deal),
- Fulfilling the terms of the contract or deal (build, make, and/or do), and
- Follow up (continue the relationship).

Marketing

Review your marketing carefully.

Each different type of marketing that you do should bring in leads. Most construction companies rely on just 2 methods.

- Word of Mouth
- Referrals

It's going to be extremely difficult to grow based on those 2 tactics. That's because both of those are passive—you just wait around **hoping** that someone will call you. And then you **hope** that you'll get the deal. That's stressful!

Sometimes, business owners will remind me that they sponsor their kids' sports teams, or that they have signage on their trucks. Congratulations, you're using "branding". That gives you a grand total of 3.

If you think branding is a marketing tactic I'm going to call BS. I believe in supporting local sports but putting your name at the football stadium or baseball diamond is really just adding financial support to your favourite team.

Why do I say that? Because there's no call to action in that tactic. A call to action (or CTA) shows people how to get in touch with you.

When I teach Construction Owners about marketing, I lay out at least 72 different marketing tactics in front of you like a buffet. I want you to choose the best ideas for you and your market.

Your goal is to have 10 different marketing tactics, each bringing 10% of your new lead flow in.

Let's look at the impact of adding a new flow of leads on a business.

STORY TIME

George is a residential home painter. When I met him he was doing 2-3 small bungalows a month. His sales were less than $100k a year. He's a pretty funny guy. When I asked him how busy he was in his business he said,

"Let me put it this way, I have the best vacation schedule ever."

Here are the places he was getting his leads:

1. Referrals
2. Word of Mouth.

George felt completely stuck. He was only getting small deals and felt like he was being pushed around by price shoppers even though people knew he did good work.

I had George do the Who Am I? exercise (Chapter 1) and the Who is My Ideal Client? exercise (Chapter 5).

Then we built a Heat Map.

Next, we added just 2 new tactics:

- Local signage
- Direct mail.

Here's what happened

- Job sizes jumped from $2,500 to $8k.
- He has so much work, he uses subs for power washing.
- He drives around less because we focused him in the wealthy part of town.
- He's not a Construction Millionaire just yet, but, in 2 months, he's already about halfway there.

Watch his video interview with me and hear how he gets wealthy clients:

ConstructionMillioniareSecrets.com/George

Look at your marketing and carefully consider what you need to do. What will work best for you?

Think about how your new prospects will view your company based on your marketing.

For more on this, see the Branding section below.

Sales

Budget, need, timing, and trust have always been the 4 critical ingredients to helping somebody buy. Ask yourself if your sales literature supports these 4 major questions. If not, now is the time to make those edits!

Coaching Question from Dom:

How does your sales process build trust in the prospect?

Coaching Tip:

Show me your company values process and procedure.

In the sales process, show the customer an easy-to-understand flowchart called "How we build and install your product/service", and "How we clean and sanitize our truck, van, tools, office, etc."

Take a look at the following example.

With the COVID global pandemic, trust is a critical part of choosing a contractor.

To help build trust with the prospect, I have my clients create a very simple 1-page flyer that they can share across the kitchen table to help people trust them.

Jay runs a small crew that does construction in a resort community. He'll build your deck and docks, fix your cottage, or build you a brand new one. Here's the 1-page flyer he built to explain how his company is staying safe. Note that his real version is in color.

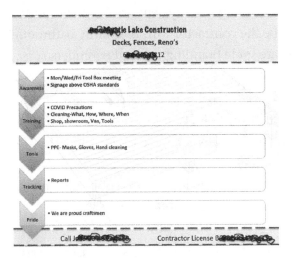

For a walkthrough of the flyer, and how Jay explains it to the customer, go to:

www.constructionmillionairesecrets.com/bonus

Branding basics

I'm going to be blunt—if your brand looks cheap, people will immediately assume you don't take care of the small things, like disinfecting tools and equipment (or yourself, for that matter).

Think about how you feel when you walk into a restaurant and their bathroom is filthy.

No matter how good the food is, you feel like you're taking a chance, right?

We're living through an absolutely unprecedented global event where safety and hygiene are front and center. Do you want to be the contractor with the "filthy bathroom"?

Here are some branding tips and reminders:

- Get a professional logo. Use Fiverr.com or Upwork.com to find an artist to make it for you.
- Your logo needs to look clean and crisp—get high-resolution images.
- It needs to look good in black, color, and greyscale.
- A simple, clean logo is always best.

An easy branding win is to have your business cards printed on the heaviest, thickest stock you can get.

This *tiny* investment will pay massive dividends by building trust and credibility.

Print them on VistaPrint.com and choose the Ultra Thick cards. They are only $40 for 100. Do not get Premium—halfway won't cut it anymore.

Have t-shirts and golf shirts made for you and your company. Your crew needs to wear those t-shirts at work everyday. Put your logo on a hi-vis t-shirt and you have PPE as well as branding all in 1 shot

Put your logo on your truck. Wrapping a vehicle can be expensive so start with high-quality graphics stickers on the doors and back. Make sure your logo is visible, and your phone number is easy to read from 25 feet away.

Create lawn signs. Put them on the customer's lawn as soon as you start a job, and ask if you can leave it up for a while. Make sure your logo is easy to read and your phone number or email address are easy to read from 25 feet away.

Appointment-setting

The highest producing, most professional, consultative salespeople understand that appointment-setting is the most critical part of guaranteeing a smooth buying process ("making the sale" in the old way of saying things).

Remember, there is absolutely no selling allowed during the appointment-setting stage. This step in the sales process has 1 perfect outcome. That outcome is getting a **qualified appointment** with **all decision-makers** at a **pre-set time and place**.

Trying to sell at this stage is a rookie mistake and you will lose this deal.

However, you'll still need to ask great questions and be prepared to answer their questions.

Fortunately, we already know what their questions will be! They will ask you questions around the following 4 topics:

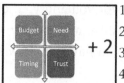 + 2

1. Budget,
2. Need,
3. Timing, and
4. Trust,

- Plus, they'll always have 2 technical, industry-specific questions.

Think back to high school or university. How happy would you have been if the teacher told you all of the questions that were going to be on the exam?

Imagine how well you would have done in school!

Well, here we are in the real world and our dreams have come true. When everything is on the line (helping this deal come together) we already know the questions on the exam!

Sales presentation

The same 4 questions that our prospect asked during appointment-setting will come up during the sales presentation. I'll explain more about this below.

Handling objections

In the old way of selling, objections felt random and were often difficult to deal with. That's because we didn't understand the 4 ingredients to helping somebody make a buying decision.

In the new method, when we help people buy, we already know the objections our (pending) customer will have. They're always around the 4 areas of budget, need, timing, and trust, as well as 2 technical, industry-specific questions they will have.

Follow-ups

Sometimes we don't get the agreement on the first visit. When that happens, we get sent to the wild country of **Follow-up-istan!**

Follow-up-istan is a cold and lonely place, and there's no sure way out of it. But **you've already come this far, so you need to try to salvage the deal**.

Here are some tricks to help you make it across the border and still get the deal.

* Use a standard, pre-written but customizable follow-up email to send after the meeting.
* Send that message immediately after the failed presentation.
* Set a specific date and time to follow-up.
* 1 day after the presentation, send a flowchart or a video explaining your production process and any other systems that might build trust (workplace health and safety, hygiene, etc.).
* Follow up the way you promised to.

TRUST BREADCRUMBS

We've always needed breadcrumbs to lead people to our business.

SECRET #18: Trust Breadcrumbs help you sell.

When I talk about **Trust Breadcrumbs**, I'm talking about little tiny pieces of evidence that you are a reputable and quality company.

This could include uniforms (even just t-shirts), vehicle wrapping, wearing booties in the customer's house, quality business cards, and a solid online presence.

The internet is very helpful here, particularly in helping you get those breadcrumbs out there. Have free downloads available on your website to answer the big questions your customers have.

If you don't have a website or it hasn't been updated lately, you'll need to do that. For a website developer who knows construction, look at **ConstructionMillionaireSecrets.com/ Cody**. I work with Cody a lot. He knows his stuff and you'll come out ahead by doing it right the first time.

Of course, you already know they'll have questions in the areas of budget, need, timing, and trust.

Exercise: Help your customer buy from you

This exercise will help you build a winning sales presentation.

Have you ever noticed that customers always ask the same questions and have the same concerns?

Millionaire contractors are always looking for places to use Simple Systems, and the selling process is a perfect example of that. Let's build your Simple System for answering every customer question and winning every job you want.

Exercise: Help Your Customer Buy From You

Instructions:

Print this exercise from:

www.constructionmillionairesecrets.com/bonus

Budget

Write the 3 most common and tough questions you get about money or budget . . .

Question 1

Question 2

Question 3

Now → write out the best answers you can give:

Answer 1

Answer 2

Answer 3

Need

Write the 3 most common and tough questions you get about why someone even needs what you do or make . . .

Question 1

Question 2

Question 3

Now → write out the best answers you can give, here:

Answer 1

Answer 2

Answer 3

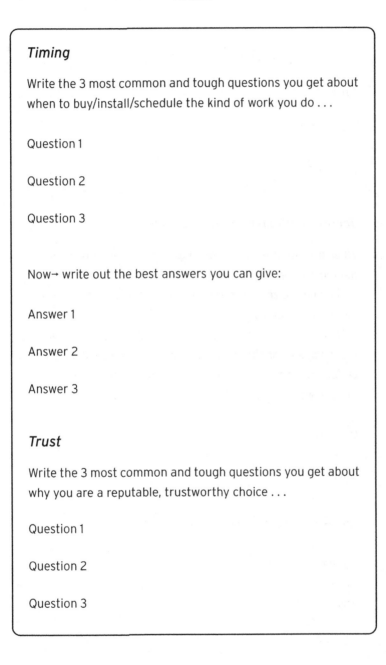

Timing

Write the 3 most common and tough questions you get about when to buy/install/schedule the kind of work you do . . .

Question 1

Question 2

Question 3

Now→ write out the best answers you can give:

Answer 1

Answer 2

Answer 3

Trust

Write the 3 most common and tough questions you get about why you are a reputable, trustworthy choice . . .

Question 1

Question 2

Question 3

Now → write out the best answer you can give:

Answer 1

Answer 2

Answer 3

Technical, industry-specific questions

What are the 2 technical or industry specific questions you get most often?

Each trade and sometimes even different services will have different questions.

For example, you might hear questions about hot water tanks vs. air conditioning systems, but you're still in HVAC. Or for cabinetmakers, you get different questions about commercial work than for kitchens.

Question 1

Question 2

Now → write out the best answers you can give:

Answer 1

Answer 2

Congratulations! You now know every possible question you could possibly get asked by a new customer.

Even better, you also have the perfect answer. Print a copy of these answers so you can refer to it the next time you're in a sales situation. You're now unstoppable.

CHAPTER 6

TAKE ACTION

"When you pray, move your feet."

I've heard that line as part of a joke and I've heard it in the boardroom of a man who is very strong in his faith.

But when I do my research to find the original source, it's hard to say where this phrase came from.

No matter where it came from or who said it first, the point is the same: you can't just think about things, you have to take action to make them come true.

SIMPLE SYSTEMS AND YOUR MINDSET

I know this sounds way too easy, but the reason we use Simple Systems is because they're easy to remember!

As a growth mindset business owner, you have a lot on your mind.

That's why a Construction Millionaire relies on a few simple and very powerful rules to live and work by.

Getting complicated, getting fancy, and making long SOPs or flowcharts that no one will ever look at is a recipe for failure.

I interviewed Nick Slavik, a residential painter—and a Construction Millionaire—for the podcast.

He started solo and now has 20 employees and annual sales well over $2 million.

He and I were talking about putting systems in place for the business.

During the interview he blurted out,

"Creating a process only takes seconds–not hours, not days, not weeks, not months."

In saying that, he touched on another secret.

SECRET #19: If you spend over 5 minutes writing out a system, you're taking too long.

When it comes to his systems, the mindset of a Construction Millionaire should be this:

We have a system for doing X, Y, and Z, and it's written in sandstone. We follow our system until we find a better way, then we tweak the system.

At the start of your next job, create a system for something you want your guys to do consistently.

Write it on a piece of paper, hand it to everyone, and have a *3-minute* meeting about it.

What you're doing is setting your expectations for how this job will go.

If you get feedback or other great ideas, make changes as needed.

Either way, you have a perfectly created, working system in your hand. Save it to your company hard drive and make it your way of doing things each time.

Each system is another brick in the wall for building your business into a million-dollar contracting company.

YOUR LEADERSHIP AND WHAT YOU EXPECT FROM OTHERS

Your company is a reflection of you.

Your crew is watching and listening to you. What you do and don't do is what they'll do when you're not around.

All you have to do is reinforce your expectations.

Go back and read the section on Culture Training in Chapter 4. If you've realized that you need a smooth-working team to become a Construction Millionaire, then I hope you also realize you'll have to focus on your own leadership skills as well.

Now that you've mastered the technical part of your trade, it's time to become a leader of people

Here's another Construction Millionaire Secret.

SECRET #20: You can't do this alone.

If you think you can, I know how old you are—you're still young!

Working in construction is just plain *hard* on your body.

Let me ask you—how are your knees, your back, your shoulders, your hips, your fingers, or your arms?

How long can you really work *alone* at a crazy pace?

At some point, in order to grow, you need to build a team you can trust. That's why I want to remind you again that **a Construction Millionaire has a handful of *Simple* Systems**.

I've always found that the hard part is breaking it down to **just a few rules**.

You've seen these already and I'm repeating them here on purpose—remember, have a handful of rules and stick to them like a dog on a bone, right?

Because the leadership mindset is a huge part of being a Construction Millionaire.

Say this out loud:

"My leadership mindset is a huge part of being a Construction Millionaire."

CONCLUSION

Let's recap what we've learned. Here are the Construction Millionaire Secrets I want you to take away from this book.

The Construction Millionaire Secrets

1. You need to understand your *why*.

2. You have to start thinking, acting, planning, and goal-setting as if your RR/h is $400 per hour.

3. Keep it simple.

4. Make a strategic plan, stick to it, and follow it.

5. You have to look at the playing field differently than everyone else.

6. Know the Customer Formula, Revenue Formula, and Profit Formula, when to use them, and how to use them together.

---

7. Get recurring revenue.

8. Always choose attitude first.

9. Construction Millionaires train everybody the same.

10. Find a way to know that your directions are followed.

11. Create a handful of simple rules, tell your crew what they are, and stick to them like a dog to a bone.

12. You need to become a businessperson who happens to run a contracting business, not a contractor with a crew.

13. There's no one else in this world who can limit your success—only *you*.

14. Construction Millionaires are wise—they grow slowly and deliberately.

15. You need to be a lion in a room full of zebras.

16. Use Heat Maps to find and price residential work.

17. Trust will be the main driving factor in making buying decisions.

18. Trust Breadcrumbs help you sell.

19. If you spend over 5 minutes writing out a system, you're taking too long.

20. You can't do this alone.

If you like and agree with these secrets, take them and make them your own—they're the rules that show you cracks of light in the darkness.

www.constructionmillionairesecrets.com/bonus

These are the secrets multi-generational millionaire business owners talk to their kids about at the kitchen table. I only got them down in these pages after 20 years of building construction businesses for my clients.

At my kitchen table, we talked about work ethic, about keeping your word. We talked about keeping promises. We talked about having pride in our work. And we talked about being a good employee.

But, I had to go find these secrets of business ownership and building million-dollar companies on my own.

I took training. I invested in courses. I learned things and put them in place. I failed, then I worked hard to fix my failures. I said the wrong things, then I worked hard to say it right the next time. I did things the wrong way, then I did them again until I got it right.

I watched my clients. I showed them how to put winning ideas in place. Then I watched them win.

The things you've learned in this book are the kind of Construction Millionaire Secrets that don't get taught in school.

I had to learn these the hard way. I learned by failing and then figuring out how to fix my failures. I learned by winning and working like a madman to repeat the steps to win again.

I watch for wisdom and I remember the lessons wise people have taught me. And I've had the opportunity to learn faster by working with so many companies at the same time.

I want to return to something we talked about in Chapter 4. Talking about teams, I showed you the following rules and told you to make these the rules for earning a spot on your team—and being able to *stay* on your team.

- **Positive**: I speak positively and I look for solutions. Leave the negative talk for negative people.
- **Responsibility**: I know that I am responsible for everything I do, think, and say. I take that responsibility seriously.
- **Ownership:** I always do my best. I might make a different decision than somebody else but I will stand behind that decision. If you disagree, ask me to explain myself.

Do that.

But also take these rules for *yourself*. Becoming a Construction Millionaire begins and ends with your mindset.

Nobody in this world can limit your success—nobody but *you*.

Give me 1 more second to tell you the reason I do what I do—my *why* from your Chapter 1 exercise.

I'm a dad. I'm a husband. I'm a son and a brother. Taking care of my family is what drives me. I believe that I'm here to take care of the people around me.

And—before social distancing threw a wrench in my plans—I would tell you that it's my job on this Earth to do so much good while I'm here that when I die, the church will be absolutely packed and overflowing at my funeral.

I guess I need a new measurement now, but I hope you get the point

Thanks for reading,

Dom

Dominic Rubino

HOW TO GET
MORE HELP . . .

THE PODCASTS

Many years ago, a cabinetry association asked if they could record my presentation for members who weren't able to show up.

That recording eventually became a podcast.

To keep a very long story short, I now host 2 different construction trades podcasts.

(Before you read these descriptions, it's important to know that both of these shows have ZERO technical talk. They're both about the *business* of construction and contracting.)

The Profit Tool Belt Podcast

This show is for construction and contracting business owners. I interview guests and discuss the hot topics in construction. It's all about tips, shortcuts, and great ideas from other business owners—how they're dealing with things like time, team, money, sales, business operations, and even family business issues.

This show was recently named 1 of the top 15 construction podcasts in the world.

The Cabinet Maker Profit System Podcast

This is the show that started it all. I interview industry experts and guests in the finished wood trades industry. We have listeners from all over the English-speaking world who run shops in cabinetry, architectural millwork, furniture, and specialty wood applications (think of surfboards, antique restoration, elevator panels, wine racks, and Murphy beds).

HOW TO ACCESS YOUR BONUSES

Throughout this book, you found several free bonuses. For quick reference, here is a list of the videos, worksheets, and other bonus resources mentioned in the book.

The **Who Am I?** worksheet: Use this free tool to get really clear on who you are, what your company's about, and who you want to be. Download it here:

www.constructionmillionairesecrets.com/bonus

The **What Is My WHY?** worksheet: This is like a compass for your business. This is the exercise for you (and your partner) to get really clear on why you do what you do. This will help you figure out the deep motivations that really drive you. Download it here:

www.constructionmillionairesecrets.com/bonus

Calculate your **Revenue Responsibility per Hour:** For a simple worksheet to calculate your RR/h or share it with a partner, go to:

www.constructionmillionairesecrets.com/bonus

Print your own **2-finger MBA:** A fun reminder that you don't need a college diploma or university degree to build an empire. If that were true, professors would all be driving Ferraris. Post this in your office—or show it to your mom!

www.constructionmillionairesecrets.com/bonus

The Construction Millionaire Formula: This is Secret #6 (so you can get Secrets #13 and #2 to work for you). The Construction Millionaire Formula is THE turnaround tool that helped me build my own multimillion-dollar companies, and show others how to do it, too. Download it here:

www.constructionmillionairesecrets.com/bonus

List of job site expectations: This is a list you can print, customize, and share with your team to make your wishes crystal clear. Download it here:

www.constructionmillionairesecrets.com/bonus

Sales are down, but profit is up 385%: To see Matt's text message about his incredible 385% profit increase, go to:

www.constructionmillionairesecrets.com/bonus

George's Story: George took his average job from $2,500 to $8k, and now he's as busy as he wants to be. See how he uses marketing to focus on wealthy clients at:

www.constructionmillionairesecrets.com/bonus

How to use a 1-page flyer to build trust and close the best deals: I'll walk you through a 1-page flyer used by a contractor in a small resort town. He uses it to show how his company relies on Simple Systems and processes to keep clients safe during the COVID-19 pandemic. Clients love it because it answers all the questions they have about choosing the right contractor for their cottage reno. See it here:

www.constructionmillionairesecrets.com/bonus

How to sell like a pro and win every job you want: It's like having all the questions on the exam *before* you walk in to take the test! Download the worksheet here:

www.constructionmillionairesecrets.com/bonus

WEBSITES REFERENCED

BusinessKnowHow.com—This is the survey where only 7% of all the businesses in the USA have sales over $1 million.

BiggerPockets.com—Excellent podcast and website for finding real estate investors so that you can work on their properties. As an added bonus, this is a great place to learn about investing for yourself.

Fiverr.com—Use this site to find contractors who can help you with 1-time office and admin tasks.

Upwork.com—Use this site to find contractors for more complicated, ongoing projects.

VistaPrint.com—I like using this online printer because it saves me time.

Join the free Facebook group—Search for the "Contractor Strategy Group" on Facebook. This is a business-owner-only group where we talk about the things that matter to us. You'll have to complete the application before approval.

SPEAK WITH US

If you'd like some help from my team to put these ideas in place and ultimately grow your construction business, I'd like to invite you to speak with us.

Just go to:

www.constructionmillionairesecrets.com/bonus

Once you fill in the short application, my team and I will take care of all the details.

Don't be shy—tell me everything about your business or your business idea. I want to be well-prepared for our meeting.

Once you answer the questions, look at my calendar openings and choose a time that works best for you.

Once you've booked your time, the confirmation page will have instructions on how to prepare for our meeting. Please review them thoroughly. You'll also find case studies from our clients and hear how others have put these ideas in place.

I made a video that breaks down what working together will look like, so you'll have a few hours or days to carefully consider this and the impact it will have on you and your company. That way, when you get on the call, many of your questions will already have been answered.

On our call, you and I will take a look at what you're doing, identify any problems and bottlenecks, and see if I can help. If I can, I'll show you what it would look like to work with us. You decide if you want to become one of my clients.

There's no pressure from my side, but either way, you'll get a lot of value and certainly some great ideas and direction out of this call.

Visit **www.constructionmillionairesecrets.com/bonus** to book your call today.

ACKNOWLEDGEMENTS

I want to thank all of the brave and rugged business people I have learned from that have helped me get to where I am today.

When I left the corporate world I didn't know where I would end up. After 20 years of private, confidential meetings behind closed doors with the smartest, most passionate and driven business owners anyone could ever meet, I have listened and learned as much as I have taught and shared.

To those of you who I have cut out of my life because of your small thinking, lack of integrity, blame, excuses, denial, and inability to keep up—see ya!

With a deep sigh of relief and a huge high-5, my thanks go to Cody Neer for helping me get focussed on this as a business and for pushing me to finally write this book.

To my assistant, Jaira, you've been invaluable (and patient!) Thank-you!

To my Editor, Conor McCarthy, thanks for your guidance and insight in helping this come together.

ACKNOWLEDGEMENTS

I want to thank Marty Park for being my longest-standing friend and business mentor over the years. You help me add Zeros' to my life. You have been in the wings as I built both of my mega-corps and you've always been there. I'm here for you too. You are a wise man, and a true friend—and that is the highest praise I can give anyone.

Above all else, and first, I have to thank Diedre for saying yes to being my wife. Having a life and family with you is simply the best. I call you "Tenacious D" for a reason! You are never flustered, you never fail, and you also never laugh at my crazy ideas and creative ranting.

Ti Amo, Schmiedera.

CONNECT WITH DOM

Profit Tool Belt Podcast

Cabinet Maker Profit System Podcast

REFERENCES

Brian Tracy, "The Way to Wealth", December, 2006
Sun Tsuh, "The Art of War", November 1, 2007
Archimedes, 6 Simple Machines, 300BC

ABOUT THE AUTHOR

Dominic Rubino started his first company to fill time between the end of exams and Christmas. He installed Christmas lights on people's homes and called it the Yo Ho Ho Light Co. At the end of his first year his net profit was $27.

And he was hooked on business ownership.

Since then, Dominic has gone on to build and sell 2 multi-million-dollar businesses from scratch. He has also been the professional business coach for hundreds of privately held companies around the world. He spoke on the TED Talk stage, he has written for Forbes, PROFIT Magazine, various trade magazines and been featured on national business radio programs.

Dominic sold his last company because he was travelling far too much and not seeing his family. He has started 2 construction podcasts as a way to help construction business owners find ways to work smarter . . . not just harder.

He is a board advisor to select companies and a business coach to growth-minded business owners. All of this has been done without any outside financing, funding, bank money, or family loans.

Dominic believes that he is here to change the world. His favourite quote is:

_____

"I want to throw enough value at the world that I'm happy with what I get from the overspray"

_____

Made in United States
North Haven, CT
27 January 2024

47997635R00095